Billy the Kid's Grave

A History of the Wild West's Most Famous Death Marker

First Edition

David G. Thomas

Mesilla Valley History Series, Vol 4

Copyright © 2017 by Doc45 Publishing

All Rights Reserved

This book, or parts thereof, may not be reproduced in any form,
including information storage and retrieval systems,
without explicit permission from Doc45 Publishing,
except for brief quotations included in articles and reviews.

For further information, please address
Doc45 Publishing, P. O. Box 5044, Las Cruces, N. M. 88003
books@doc45.com

To obtain printed or ebooks, visit:
doc45.com

Cover artwork by Dusan Arsenic.

ISBN 978-1-542-40472-3

Contents

Acknowledgements iv

1. Killing Billy – "Kid Talked Before He Shot" 1
   Trial and Escape 1
   The Hunt 8
   Why Did Billy Not Leave the Area? 9
   Who Was Billy's Girlfriend? 10
   Killed 13
   Fateful Choice 16
   Justifiable Homicide 18
   Dead or Alive 18
   Press Response 20
   "The Authentic Life of Billy the Kid" 21
   Photos 23

2. Billy's Grave – "The Bivouac of the Dead" 41
   Billy's Burial 41
   The Cost of Fame 42
   Paulita's Midnight Visit 44
   The First Tourist 44
   Fort Sumner Abandoned 45
   Billy's Grave Misplaced in Public Imagination 45
   Cemetery Flooded 46
   Garrett Revisits Billy's Grave 46
   Soldiers Moved from the Cemetery 48
   Fred E. Sutton Visits the Cemetery 49
   "The Saga of Billy the Kid" 50
   Fort Sumner in 1926 50
   Marking Billy's Grave 51
   Locating Billy's Grave 52
   King Vidor's BILLY THE KID 53
   Billy's Grave Marked 53
   Fort Sumner in 1937 55
   Cemetery Sold For Taxes and Plowed 55
   Billy Gets His Own Marker 58
   Lucien Bonaparte Maxwell Given a Stone 59
   Billy's Marker Stolen 59
   Lawsuit War to Move Billy to Lincoln 60
   Fort Sumner Park Created 63
   Billy's Marker Returned 63
   Billy's Marker Stolen Again 64

2.   Billy's Grave – "The Bivouac of the Dead" (cont'd)

     Is Billy's Grave in the Right Location? 65

     Was Billy Really Killed? 66

     Photos 69

3. Cemetery Burials 95

     Military Burials 96

     Maxwell Family 97

     Bonney, Bowdre, and O'Folliard 100

     Abreu Family 101

     Beaubien Family 102

     Foor Family 103

     Garcia Family 103

     Gonzales Family 104

     Harris Family 104

     Jaramillo Family 105

     Sandoval Family 105

     Silva Family 105

     Anaya Family 106

     Baca Family 106

     Gallegos Family 106

     Lobato [Lovato] Family 106

     Madrid Family 106

     Mares Family 107

     Pena Family 107

     Salguero Family 107

     Segura Family 107

     Velasquez Family 107

     Zamora Family 107

     Other Burials 107

     Photos 110

Appendix A – Charles W. Dudrow's Correspondence 129

Appendix B – Interview with Sheriff Pat Garrett 133

Notes 135

Index 141

Mesilla Valley History Series

La Posta – From the Founding of Mesilla, to Corn Exchange Hotel, to Billy the Kid Museum, to Famous Landmark – by David G. Thomas

Giovanni Maria de Agostini, Wonder of The Century – The Astonishing World Traveler Who Was A Hermit – by David G. Thomas

Screen with a Voice – A History of Moving Pictures in Las Cruces, New Mexico – by David G. Thomas

Billy the Kid's Grave – A History of the Wild West's Most Famous Death Marker – by David G. Thomas

Killing Garrett, The Wild West's Most Famous Lawman – Murder or Self-Defense? – by David G. Thomas

The Stolen Pinkerton Reports of Colonel Albert J. Fountain Investigation — David G. Thomas, Editor

Doc 45

Buenas noches boys,
A social call no doubt –
Do we talk it over,
Or do we shoot it out?

I'm Doc 45,
Toughest man alive.
Hand over those golden bills
Or I'll dose you up with dirty leaden pills.

Dedicated To

Joe Lopez

Friend, artist, and historian. You left this world too early.

Acknowledgements

I thank Aaron J. Roth, Site Manager, Bosque Redondo Memorial, Fort Sumner, New Mexico, for help in locating documents; Kerri Webb, Deputy Court Clerk, De Baca County, for help in researching court cases; Thayla Wright, librarian, Arthur Johnson Memorial Library, Raton, New Mexico; staff, Fort Sumner Public Library; Tim Sweet, Billy the Kid Museum; Lori Ann Goodloe, Billy the Kid Outlaw Gang; and Dan Aranda for editing, proofing, and fact-checking.

Special thanks to Scott Smith, Coronado Historic Site, Bernalillo, New Mexico for permission to quote from his letter regarding the location of Billy the Kid's grave.

For photographs and permission to use them, I thank the Arizona Historical Society; New Mexico State University Special Collections; Palace of the Governors (NMHM); University of Arizona Special Collections; Center for Southwest Research and Special Collections; Arthur Johnson Memorial Library; Indiana State Historical Society, and Fort Sumner Public Library.

Unattributed photos are from the author's collection.

Billy the Kid, real name William Henry McCarty. Photo believed to have been taken at Fort Sumner in 1880.

Introduction

Several days after completing this manuscript, I went on a long-planned vacation to Southeast Asia. While there, I learned that I needed open heart surgery. I returned to the United States and underwent the surgery in Dallas.

It was a challenging experience. I was in the hospital for over a month, during which I often reflected on the substantial impact the care and compassion I received from the hospital staff had on my attitude and feelings.

As the text of this book was still occupying my mind, I began to think about how Billy the Kid's childhood experiences may have affected his character. Most historians believe he was born in New York in 1859. His Father is unknown. Many have speculated that his Mother may not have been married. Billy, his younger brother Joseph, and his Mother Catherine McCarty left New York in 1872 for Wichita, Kansas. There they moved onto a farm owned by William H. Antrim, who later would become Billy's stepfather. Catherine and her sons were probably taken on by Antrim as a charity case, and as free farm labor.[1] Within a few months, Antrim and his three wards left Kansas for New Mexico, where Antrim married Catherine in Santa Fe on March 1, 1873. [2]

Shortly after the marriage, the new family moved to Silver City, New Mexico.[3] There, on September 16, 1874, Catherine died of tuberculosis.

> *Died in Silver City, on Wednesday the 16th inst., Catherine, wife of William Antrim, aged 45 years.*
>
> *Mrs. Antrim with her husband and family came to Silver City about one year and a half ago, since which time her health has not been good, having suffered from an affection of the lungs, for the last four months she had been confined to her bed. The funeral occurred from the family residence, on Main street, at 2 o'clock, on Thursday. [4]*

One year after his Mother's death, Billy was arrested and jailed for stealing. Billy was manipulated into hiding goods stolen by George Shaffer, a much older tough known around Silver City as "Sombrero Jack."

> *Henry McCarty, who was arrested on Thursday [Sept 23] and committed to jail to await the action of the grand jury, upon the charge of stealing clothes from Charley Sun and Sam Chung, celestials, sans cue, sans Josa [Joss] sticks, escaped from prison yesterday through the chimney. It's believed that Henry was simply the tool of "Sombrero Jack," who done the stealing whilst Henry done the hiding. Jack has skinned out. [5]*

Following his escape from the jail, Billy fled Silver City, beginning his now famous life as an adult.

2 ~ Introduction

From this brief account (all that is possible here), it is evident that Billy's childhood produced a hard and self-reliant individual. With a missing natural Father, and a Mother who died when he was 15, Billy had little exposure to the softer influences provided by a loving family. Just before Billy was killed, he was pursuing a sweetheart and probable lover, as discussed in this text. If he had not been killed, and had obtained his goal of a mate, he would likely have become a different man, and may well have spent the rest of his life as a law-abiding citizen. It was not to be.

This book is divided into three chapters. The first gives an account of the chain of events that led directly to Billy's death, beginning with the singular event that started the sequence, Billy's conviction for murder and his sentencing to hang. As much as possible, these events are related using the actual words of witnesses and contemporaries. The second chapter tells the story of Billy's burial and the many surprising incidents associated with his grave over the years. The third chapter lists the 111 men and women known to be buried along with Billy in the Fort Sumner cemetery, with short biographies where possible. Sixteen of these individuals had very direct connections with Billy. Appendix A supplies Charles W. Dudrow's correspondence regarding the locating and disinterring of the military burials at Fort Sumner. Appendix B reprints the only newspaper interview ever granted by Sheriff Patrick F. Garrett on the killing of Billy the Kid.

Note: For those unfamiliar with New Mexico, references in the text to Las Vegas refer to Las Vegas, New Mexico. References to Fort Sumner are always to the military fort, unless explicitly specified otherwise.

Chapter 1 | Killing Billy – "Kid Talked Before He Shot"

"Quien es?"

The reply to this incautious question – "Who is it?" – was a bullet to the heart.

That bullet – fired by Lincoln County Sheriff Patrick F. Garrett from a .40-44 caliber single action Colt revolver – ended the life of Billy the Kid, real name William Henry McCarty.

The events leading to Billy the Kid's death were as follows:

Trial and Escape

On April 28, 1881, Billy escaped from confinement in the Lincoln County Courthouse, where he had been taken to be hung, following his conviction for first degree murder in the county courthouse of Mesilla, New Mexico:

> **"Territory of New Mexico vs. William Bonney, alias 'Kid', alias William Antrim"**
>
> *"Now comes the plaintiff herein by Simon B. Newcomb, Esq., District Attorney therefore and the Defendant appearing in his own proper person and accompanied by John D. Bail Esq., and A. J. Fountain Esq. his attorneys, and the Jury empanelled (sic) yesterday in said cause being present and said jury having heard all the evidence and the arguments of council and received the instructions of the Court, retire to deliberate, accompanied by two sworn officers and after deliberation the said Jury return into Court and upon their oaths do say: 'We the Jury in the above entitled cause do find the Defendant guilty of murder in the first degree and do assess his punishment at death.'"*
>
> *"April 9, 1881"* [1]

Billy's conviction was for killing Lincoln County Sheriff William Brady on April 1, 1878. The territorial laws of New Mexico mandated that the punishment for first degree murder be death by hanging. Thus, the jury had no choice in assessing the punishment, in spite of the suggestion of such by the last words of the verdict.[2]

Accordingly, four days later, presiding Judge Warren Henry Bristol issued the following sentence:

> *"It is therefore considered by the Court here that the said defendant, William Bonny (sic), alias Kid, alias William Antrim, be taken to the County of Lincoln, in the Third Judicial District of the Territory of New Mexico, by the Sheriff of the County of Doña Ana in said Judicial District and Territory and there by him delivered into the custody of the Sheriff of the said County of Lincoln, and that he, the said William Bonny, alias Kid, alias William Antrim, be confined in prison in said County of Lincoln by the Sheriff of such County until on Friday, the 13th day of May, in the Year of our Lord One Thousand Eight Hundred and Eighty-One."*

"That on the day aforesaid, between the hours of nine of the clock in the forenoon and three of the clock in the afternoon, he, the said William Bonny, alias Kid, alias William Antrim, be taken from such prison to some suitable and convenient place of execution within said County of Lincoln, by the Sheriff of said County, and that then and there on that day and between the aforesaid hours thereof by the Sheriff of said County of Lincoln, he, the said William Bonny, alias Kid, alias William Antrim, be hanged by the neck until his body be dead." [3]

Billy was ordered to Lincoln to hang, rather than hung in Mesilla, because Lincoln was where the crime was committed.

The most influential territorial press, the *Santa Fe Daily New Mexican,* was euphoric at the prospect of Billy's demise:

"When the Kid's execution comes off it will probably attract more people than any similar even that ever occurred in the Territory. Certainly this consideration ought to flatter and console the young gentleman." [4]

"They made short work of trying and convicting the Kid. Now if they will be as prompt with the hanging the territory will soon be rid of one of its worse characters." [5]

It took six days to get Billy the 145 miles to Lincoln. Billy and a court-appointed posse of five guards left Mesilla on the night of April 16, 1881, with Billy *"hand-cuffed and shackled and chained to the back seat of the ambulance [wagon]."* On April 21, Billy was delivered to Sheriff Garrett at Fort Stanton; the following day Garrett had him imprisoned in the Lincoln County Courthouse.[6]

Because Lincoln had no jail at the time, two upstairs rooms in the County Courthouse were being used as the town's jail. Billy was confined alone in the smaller of the two jail rooms, which was considered the most secure.[7] The larger jail room contained five prisoners judged low-risk for escaping.[8] A third upstairs room served as Sheriff Garrett's office and a place *"where were kept surplus arms."* [9]

Billy's guards were Sheriff Garrett, Deputy Sheriff James W. Bell, and Deputy Marshal Robert Olinger. Garrett noted:

"During the few days the Kid remained in confinement, I [Garrett] had several conversations with him. He appeared to have a plausible excuse for every crime charged against him, except, perhaps, the killing of Carlyle." [10]

"He expressed no enmity toward me for having been the instrument through which he was brought to justice...."

"As to his guards, he placed great confidence in Bell and appeared to take a great liking to him. Bell had been in no manner connected with the Lincoln County War and had no animosity or old grudge against the Kid...."

"As to Olinger, the case was altogether different. He and the Kid had met opposed in arms frequently during the past years of anarchy. Bob Beckwith, the bosom friend of Olinger, had been killed by the Kid at the close of the three days' fight in Lincoln. The Kid likewise charged Olinger with the killing of friends of

his. Between these two there existed a reciprocal hatred and neither attempted to disguise or conceal his antipathy from the other." [11]

Billy had a more immediate reason to despise Olinger. Olinger had been in charge of the posse that had transported Billy to Fort Stanton, and had, by several accounts, continually bullied him during the trip.[12]

On April 27, Garrett was obliged to leave Lincoln for the nearby town of White Oaks to collect county taxes, a regular duty of his sheriff's job. Bell and Olinger were left in charge of the prisoners.[13]

The next day, April 28, about 5 pm in the evening, Olinger took the prisoners from the larger jail room across the street for a meal – giving Billy precisely what he had been watching and hoping for – an ideal opportunity to escape.[14]

How Billy actually engineered the escape is unknown. Based on his investigation, Garrett gave the following account:

"At the Kid's request, Bell accompanied him down stairs and into the back corral [where the jail latrine was]. As they returned, Bell allowed the Kid to get considerably in advance. As the Kid turned on the landing of the stairs, he was hidden from Bell. He was light and active, and, with a few noiseless bounds, reached the head of the stairs, turned to the right, put his shoulder to the door of the room used as an armory (though locked, this door was well known to open by a firm push), entered, seized a six-shooter, returned to the head of the stairs just as Bell faced him on the landing of the stair-case, some twelve steps beneath, and fired. Bell turned, ran out into the corral and towards the little gate. He fell dead before reaching it." [15]

Several contemporary writers put forth an alternate explanation of the escape, based on Billy swinging his handcuffs as a bludgeon:

"[Olinger] had just gone to his supper, and Bell was sitting down on the floor, when 'Kid' approached him, talking in his pleasant way. Quick as lightning he jumped and struck Bell with his handcuffs, fracturing the skull. He immediately snatched Bell's revolver and shot him through the breast." [16]

"It seems the Kid had struck Bell over the head with the handcuffs and back of the ear also, breaking his skull and stunning him and then grabbing from Bell his revolver; and Bell, after partially recovering from the effects of the blow, started to run out of the hall and down stairs and Kid fired a shot at him which passed under Bell's arms and clear through his body. Bell ran towards the kitchen and old man Goss [Gottfried Gauss] was just coming out of it and Bell fell into his arms and expired without a word." [17]

A twist was added to this explanation by suggesting that Billy already had one hand free:

"As time passes and further facts concerning the Kid's escape comes in, the more wonderful and daring it appears. The hand-cuffs had been taken from his left hand, to allow him to eat supper. Watching an opportunity he dealt J. W.

6 ~ Chapter 1

Bell a blow with the irons on his right hand. This broke his skull and as he fell the Kid grabbed his pistol and finished the work." [18]

"At noon Olinger went to dinner and Bell exposed himself a little when 'Kid,' who could slip his handcuffs, seized Bell's pistol, knocked him down with it, and as he rose, shot him dead." [19]

Years later it was suggested that an unidentified accomplice had hidden a pistol in the outdoor latrine, which Billy retrieved and used to shoot Bell and escape. The fact that this theory was not suggested by any witness at the time, and the strong insistence in contemporary accounts that the gun that killed Bell was his own, cast serious doubt on this theory.

Gottfried Gauss, an eye-witness, offered the following account of what happened next:

"That memorable day I came out of my room, whence I had gone to light my pipe, and was crossing the yard behind the court-house, when I heard a shot fired, a tussle up the stairs in the court-house, somebody hurrying down stairs, and deputy sheriff Bell emerging from the door running toward me. He ran right into my arms, expired the same moment, and I laid him down, dead...."

"...I saw the other deputy sheriff, Olinger, coming out of the hotel opposite, with the other four or five county prisoners where they had taken their dinner. I called to him to come quick. He did so, leaving his prisoners in front of the hotel. When he had come close up to me, and while standing not more than a yard apart, I told him that I was just after laying Bell dead on the ground in the yard behind, and before he could reply, he was struck by a well directed shot fired from a window above us, and fell dead at my feet." [20]

Olinger was shot with his own shotgun, which Billy had retrieved from Garrett's office. Another account of the shooting revealed just how intensely personal Olinger's killing was for Billy:

"...Kid aimed at him through the window with a double-barreled shot gun and fired, hitting Olinger in the breast and after he fell emptied the other barrel, loaded with buck shot, in his shoulder. It is reported that the Kid then came out on the porch, broke the stock of the gun from the barrel and threw the pieces at the corpse, at the same time saying, 'You will never follow me again with that gun.'" [21]

Gauss continued:

"...Billy the Kid called to me: 'Don't run, I wouldn't hurt you – I am alone, and master, not only of the court-house, but also of the town, for I will allow nobody to come near us. You go,' he said, 'and saddle one of Judge Leonard's horses, and I will clear out as soon as I can have the shackles loosened from my legs.' With a little prospecting pick I had thrown to him through the window he was working for at least an hour, and could not accomplish more than to free one leg, and he came to the conclusion to await a better chance, tie one shackle to his waist-belt, and start out. Meanwhile I had saddled a small skittish pony

belonging to Billy Burt, as there was no other horse available, and had also, by Billy's command, tied a pair of red blankets behind the saddle...."

"When Billy went down stairs at last, on passing the body of Bell, he said, 'I'm sorry I had to kill him but couldn't help it.' On passing the body of Olinger, he gave him a tip with his boot, saying, 'You are not going to round me up again.'"

"We went out together where I had tied up the pony, and he told me to tell the owner of same, Billy Burt, that he would send it back next day. I, for my part, didn't much believe in this promise, but, sure enough, next morning, the pony arrived safe and sound, trailing a long lariat, at the court house in Lincoln." [22]

The news of Billy's escape was rapidly communicated to Garrett:

"On the 29th, I received a letter from John C. Delaney, Esq., of Fort Stanton, merely stating the fact of the Kid's escape and the killing of the guard. The same day Billy Nickey arrived from Lincoln and gave me the particulars." [23]

On April 30, Garrett returned to Lincoln. The day before a hastily-convened coroner's jury had formally ruled the two guards' killings an unjustified homicide, perpetrated by Billy the Kid. Garrett reconstructed the shooting of Bell as follows:

"It was found that Bell was hit under the right arm, the ball passing through the body and going out under the left arm. On examination it was evident that the Kid had made a very poor shot, for him, and his hitting Bell at all was a scratch. The ball had hit the wall on Bell's right, caromed, passed through his body, and buried itself in an adobe on his left. There was other proof besides the marks on the wall. The ball had surely been indented and creased before it entered the body, as these scars were filled with flesh." [24]

Billy's escape was just 15 days before his scheduled hanging – Friday, May 13, 1881 – which had been officially confirmed and ordered by Territorial Governor Lewis "Lew" Wallace when he signed Billy's death warrant on April 30, 1881.[25]

The news of Billy's escape flashed across the territory, with the Santa Fe and Las Vegas newspapers the first to report the escape. But Billy's prior exploits had been reported nationally, and his escape was big news throughout the nation. Dozens of newspapers from California to New York reported the escape, in front page stories.

Garrett expressed his feelings about the escape as follows:

"[It] was a most distressing calamity, for which I do not hold myself guiltless. The Kid's escape, and the murder of his two guards, was the result of mismanagement and carelessness, to a great extent. I knew the desperate character of the man... that he was daring and unscrupulous, and that he would sacrifice the lives of a hundred men who stood between him and liberty, when the gallows stared him in the face, with as little compunction as he would kill a coyote."

"[I] now realize how inadequate my precautions were. Yet, in self-defense, and hazarding the charge of shirking the responsibility and laying it upon dead men's shoulders, I must say that my instructions as to caution and the routine of duty were not heeded and followed." [26]

8 ~ Chapter 1

The Hunt

When Billy rode out of Lincoln, he was armed with *"two new revolvers, four belts of cartridges, and a new Winchester,"* courtesy of Garrett's office armory.[27]

His first stop was at his friend Yginio Salazar's place, west of Lincoln, where he was able to cut off the shackles that were still-attached to one leg. Billy knew that Salazar was just one of the many Lincoln county residents that he could rely on for help. As the Santa Fe newspaper put it:

"A man who came to Santa Fe yesterday from Lincoln county says that Billy the Kid has got more friends in that county than anybody. He gets all the money he wants, takes horses when he needs them, and makes no bones of going into and out of various towns." [28]

On learning of Billy's escape, Governor Wallace immediately issued a reward for his re-capture:

"$500 REWARD"

"I will pay $500 reward to any person or persons who will capture William Bonny, alias the Kid, and deliver him to any sheriff of New Mexico. Satisfactory presents of identity will be required."

"Lew Wallace"
"Governor of New Mexico" [29]

Garrett's reaction was more sanguine:

"During the weeks following the Kid's escape, I was censured by some for my seeming unconcern and inactivity in the matter of his re-arrest. I was egotistical enough to think I knew my own business best, and preferred to accomplish this duty, if possible at all, in my own way. I was constantly, but quietly, at work, seeking sure information and maturing my plans of action." [30]

Meanwhile, Billy was also tracking Garrett's actions, as reported in the press:

"The Kid says he is among friends and is all right. His friends keep him provided with newspapers and he seems well satisfied in his present quarters." [31]

Instead of fleeing to Mexico, which Garrett thought his most probable (and smartest) action, Billy stayed in the Lincoln area, splitting his time between trusted sheep camps and ranches and fairly regular visits to Fort Sumner, 140 miles northeast of Lincoln.

In 1881, Fort Sumner was no longer a government fort. The fort and an adjoining million-acre reservation for Mescalero Apache and Navajo Native Americans had been authorized in October, 1862, during the second year of the Civil War. The fort was named after Major General Edwin Vose Sumner. The reservation was called Bosque Redondo (round woods), the Spanish name for the dense scrub-brush lining the Pecos River where the reservation and fort were established. In June, 1868, the 9,000 or so Native Americans that had been relocated by military force onto the Bosque Redondo Reservation were permitted to return to reservations on their native lands.[32]

With the reservation abandoned, there was little purpose in maintaining Fort Sumner, so it was ordered sold by the Federal Government. On October, 17, 1870, Lucien

Bonaparte Maxwell bought the grounds and buildings of the fort, less the cemetery burial ground, for $5,000. He had earlier offered $700 for the property, which was rejected.[33] Accompanying Lucien Maxwell in his move to Fort Sumner were about two hundred persons: relatives, employees, tenant farmers – and their families – who had lived with or worked for Maxwell.[34]

In May, 1881, when Billy was visiting Fort Sumner, he was visiting property owned by Pete Maxwell, Lucien Maxwell's son. Pete had inherited the property when Lucien died on July 25, 1875.

Why Did Billy Not Leave the Area?

There were two reasons, one certain, one speculative.

It is certain that Billy had wide support among the Hispanic community of Lincoln County. The murder for which Billy was convicted, that of Sheriff Brady, had occurred during the two-year conflict known as the Lincoln County War. That conflict had pitted a primarily Anglo faction against a primarily Hispanic faction, although the leaders of both sides were Anglos. Billy had been on the side headed by Alexander A. McSween and John Henry Tunstall (an Englishman). The opposing side was lead by Lawrence G. Murphy and James J. Dolan.

Murphy and Dolan were part of and aligned with the "establishment" of Lincoln, the controlling political and financial powers of the county, disparaged by its opposition as the "Santa Fe Ring." McSween and Tunstall were new-comer upstarts challenging the establishment, which lead directly to the armed conflict of the Lincoln County War. Both McSween and Tunstall were murdered during the war. Sheriff Brady was aligned with Murphy and Dolan, and was essentially a pliant tool of Murphy and Dolan. Sheriff Brady's subsequent murder, for which Billy was convicted, was vengeance for Tunstall's blatantly unprovoked, vicious murder by a posse authorized by Brady.

Prior to Billy's trial, William L. Rynerson, the district attorney with jurisdiction over Lincoln County, petitioned the court to have the trial transferred to Mesilla, in Doña Ana County, because he was certain he could not get Billy convicted in Lincoln:

> *"W. L. Rynerson, District Attorney… being first duly sworn deposes and says that justice cannot be done [in] the said Territory on the trial of the said defendant, William Bonny (sic) alias 'Kid' alias William Antrim in the said County of Lincoln, for the reason that the jurors in attendance and all those liable to be summoned for the trial of said defendant, by reason of partisanship in the late and existing troubles and lawlessness in said County have so prejudiced the said jurors that they cannot fairly and impartially try the said defendant…."* [35]

The change of venue request was granted by Judge Bristol.

In Lincoln County, among most Hispanics and many Anglos, Billy was viewed as a just warrior who had fought for a just cause.

Billy was also viewed as having been unfairly prosecuted. On November 13, 1879, in an effort to end the Lincoln County War, Governor Wallace had issued a blanket pardon for all persons involved in the war, no matter how consequential their crime. Governor

10 ~ Chapter 1

Wallace's pardon covered even the high crime of murder, of which there may have been as many as 80 committed during the war:

"...the undersigned, by virtue of authority in him vested, further proclaims a general pardon for misdemeanors and offenses committed in the said County of Lincoln against the laws of the said Territory in connection with the aforesaid disorders, between the first day of February, 1878, and the date of this proclamation." [36]

But there was an exception to the pardon, one which covered only Billy and three of his companions:

"Neither shall it be pleaded by any person in bar of conviction under indictment now found and returned for any such crimes or misdemeanors...." [37]

The pardon could not be claimed by any person already indicted for a Lincoln County War crime – and the only persons who had been so indicted were Billy and his friends John Middleton, Henry Brown, and Fred Waite. Middleton, Brown, and Waite were never arrested or tried, as they quickly left the area following their indictments. The Lincoln County War was the American Wild West's most protracted gun-fight. And of all the participants in that conflict, Billy was the only person arrested and tried – an undeniable example of unequal justice.

There is likely a second reason Billy did not leave the Lincoln county area – he wanted to remain close to a girlfriend.

Who Was Billy's Girlfriend?

Four candidates have been proposed:

Deluvina Maxwell, an adopted member of the Maxwell family

Celsa (Martinez) Gutierrez, the sister of Sheriff Garrett's first wife

Abrana (Segura) Garcia, possibly Deluvina's sister

Paulita Maxwell, Pete Maxwell's younger sister

Deluvina Maxwell was a Navajo taken captive as a young child by Utes. When she was about nine years old, she was freed by Lucien Maxwell, probably by being purchased from her Native American captors. She then became a household servant and member of the Maxwell family.[38]

Undoubtedly, Deluvina had deep feelings for Billy, referring to him with endearments such as *"mi muchacho"* (my boy).[39] When asked about Billy not long before her death, she said, *"Billy the Kid was my compadre, my friend, poor Billy."* [40] But at 33, she was more than ten years older than Billy, an obvious obstacle. Her oft-expressed affectionate feelings for Billy are the sole evidence for an intimate relationship.

The candidate some historians have settled on is Celsa (Martinez) Gutierrez. If Celsa was Billy's girlfriend, there is a bizarre and concealed twist to this relationship. Celsa's maiden name was Martinez. Her father was Albino Martinez. Her sister was Juanita Martinez, who had married Pat Garrett in November, 1879. Juanita died within days of the marriage, after becoming violently ill during the marriage celebration.[41] She was buried in the Fort Sumner cemetery.

Within two months of Juanita Martinez's death, on January 14, 1880, Garrett married Apolinaria Gutierrez, daughter of Jose Dolores Gutierrez. At the time of his two marriages, Garrett was living in Fort Sumner. He was also serving as deputy sheriff of Lincoln County, having been appointed to that position just prior to his marriage to Juanita Martinez.[42]

Garrett's two witnesses in the wedding were Manuel Fernando Abreu and Alejandro Segura. Manuel Abreu was at Fort Sumner when Billy was killed and saw the body. Alejandro Segura was the Justice of the Peace on the coroner's jury that ruled Billy's killing justifiable homicide.[43]

How more intimate with and knowledgeable of the community around Fort Sumner could Garrett be?

He lived there, married the daughter of one Fort Sumner area family, and then when she died, married the daughter of a second Fort Sumner area family. In addition, his business as deputy sheriff was to know what was going on within the community.

In May, 1881 – when Garrett was hunting for Billy – Celsa Martinez was Celsa Gutierrez, having married Sabal Gutierrez four years earlier. If Billy's girlfriend in Fort Sumner was Celsa (Martinez) Gutierrez, then Garrett was hunting for someone who was in a likely intimate relationship with his first wife's sister – in an area he knew well, among people he knew well – something he gave no hint of in his written account of searching for Billy.

One of Garrett's deputies at the time of the search, John William Poe, does allude to this undisclosed knowledge:

> *"Garrett seemed to have but little confidence in our being able to accomplish the object of our trip, but said that he knew the location of a certain house occupied by a woman in Fort Sumner which the Kid had formerly frequented...."* [44]

Celsa was living with her husband Sabal Gutierrez, and they had a four year old daughter, Mauricia.[45] It seems unlikely that Sabal would tolerate a relationship of any degree of intimacy between his wife and Billy. In addition, Sabal was a loyal friend of Billy.

(**Note:** There were two Celsa Gutierrez's in Fort Sumner in May, 1881. Numerous writers have confused the two. Celsa (Martinez) Gutierrez, Billy's possible girlfriend, was 23 in 1881. Her parents were Albino and Feliciana Martinez. Celsa (Martinez) Gutierrez becomes a Gutierrez by marrying Sabal Gutierrez. The second Celsa Gutierrez was also 23 in 1881. Her parents were Jose Dolores and Feliciana Gutierrez. Their mothers had the same first name. Celsa Gutierrez is the sister of Apolinaria Gutierrez, Garrett's second wife. Thus, the often repeated statement that Billy's girlfriend was Garrett's wife's sister is a misidentification.)

The third candidate for girlfriend is Abrana (Segura) Garcia. Current descendents of Abrana report that, like Dcluvina Maxwell, she was a Navajo who had been captured by Utes and then freed; she may have been a younger sister of Deluvina. She was raised by Fernando and Manuel Segura as Abrana Segura.[46]

12 ~ Chapter 1

In 1880, Abrana was 22 years old and married to Martin Garcia. Living with Abrana and Martin were three children, aged seven years, five years, and five months. The two oldest children were Martin's children from a previous relationship.[47]

There is a long tradition among the descendents of Abrana (Segura) Garcia that she was Billy's girlfriend, and even that she had a son by him.[48]

The last candidate, Paulita Maxwell, is the only one suggested by a contemporary public source:

> *"It is stated that Billy was hanging around Maxwell's place for the purpose of courting Maxwell's sister, who had captured his heart."* [49]

When, in later life, Paulita was asked if this was true, she denied it:

> *"An old story that identifies me as Billy the Kid's sweetheart... has been going the rounds for many years. Perhaps it honors me; perhaps not; it depends on how you feel about it. But I was not Billy the Kid's sweetheart. I liked him very much – oh, yes – but I did not love him."* [50]

This denial, printed in Walter Noble Burns' 1926 book, *"The Saga of Billy the Kid,"* was not questioned by Burns in his book, which led to its general acceptance by subsequent historians. But in recent years, Burns' original manuscript has become available. In the original manuscript, Burns preceded Paulita's denial with statements by several people affirming that she was Billy's girlfriend. These included her sister, Odila Maxwell Abreu, who stated:

> *"There is no secret about it. Billy the Kid was madly in love with Paulita."* [51]

Poe is quoted as telling Burns:

> *"Paulita Maxwell was awakened by the shot that killed her sweetheart. It was generally reported that she and the Kid were to be married and I was rather surprised that she showed little emotion when she stood beside his dead body."* [52]

Burns removed these statements from the published version of the book at the request of his publisher, who was concerned about liability for libel.

Additional evidence for the relationship is provided by a letter written by James W. Southwick, who was the sheriff in Mesilla at the time Billy was convicted of murdering Brady. Southwick wrote that when Billy:

> *"...was in jail he showed me a letter from his girl a Miss Maxwell and that she was very much struck on Billy...."* [53]

In a second letter, he wrote *"I suppose the Miss Maxwell was the daughter of Pete Maxwell...."* [54] He meant, of course, the daughter of Lucien Maxwell (or the sister of Pete Maxwell).

After denying a "sweetheart" relationship with Billy, Paulita told Burns:

> *"Billy the Kid, after his escape at Lincoln, came to Fort Sumner, it is true, to see a woman he was in love with. But it was not I. Pat Garrett ought to have*

known who she was because he was connected with her, and not very distantly, by marriage." [55]

This is a not-so-veiled reference to Celsa (Martinez) Gutierrez. This may be simple misdirection; or it may indicate that Billy had a second or earlier relationship.

Killed

That Billy was killed on a moon-lit night at approximately 11:30 in the evening of July 14, 1881, is astonishing.

Garrett was only half-heartedly seeking him – and Billy was determined, vigilant, and among fiercely protective friends.

Forty-four days after Billy's escape, on July 11, Garrett was motivated – finally – to visit the Fort Sumner area, to hunt for Billy. His ostensible justification was a letter from Manuel S. Brazil, an informant:

"Brazil's letter gave me no positive information. He said he had not seen the Kid since his escape, but, from many indications, believed he was still in the country. He offered me any assistance in his power to recapture him." [56]

Although supplying nothing *"positive,"* Garrett arranged to meet Brazil three days later at Taiban Arroyo, an uninhabited site five miles south of Fort Sumner, taking two deputies with him, John William Poe and Thomas C. "Kip" McKinney.[57]

Brazil did not show at the meeting, so Garrett sent Poe into Fort Sumner to see what he could discover:

"In pursuance of this plan, I [Poe] next morning left my companions and rode into town, where I arrived about ten o'clock...."

"When I entered the town, I noticed I was being watched from every side, and soon after I had stopped and hitched my horse in front of a store which had a saloon annex, a number of men gathered around and began to question me as to where I was from, where bound, etc. I answered with as plausible a yarn as I was able to give...." [58]

Poe spent some time in the saloon, bought himself a *"square meal,"* and sought to extract intelligence on Billy's whereabouts:

"...but was unable to learn anything further than that the people with whom I conversed were still suspicious of me, and it was plain that many of them were on the alert, expecting something to happen." [59]

His Fort Sumner mission a failure, Poe then visited the nearby town of Sunnyside, seven miles north of Fort Sumner. There, he met with Milnor Rudulph, who invited him to have supper at his ranch:

"After supper was over, I engaged in conversation with [Rudolph], discussing the conditions in the country generally, and after some little time, I led up to the escape of Billy the Kid from Lincoln, and remarked that I had heard a report that the Kid was hiding in or about Fort Sumner. Upon my making this remark, the old gentleman showed plainly that he was getting nervous; said that he had heard that such a report was about, but did not believe it...." [60]

14 ~ Chapter 1

Leaving Rudolph, Poe rejoined Garrett and McKinney at Glorieta, a tiny settlement four miles north of Fort Sumner, as had been pre-arranged:

"I rode directly to the point where I had agreed to meet my companions, and, strange to say, as I approached the point from one direction, they came into view from the other, so that we did not have to wait for each other." [61]

Here Garrett's and Poe's accounts differ. Garrett says:

"[After hearing Poe's report] I concluded to go and have a talk with Pete Maxwell, in whom I felt I could rely." [62]

But Poe in his account claims the decision to question Pete Maxwell was his:

"I then proposed that, before leaving, we should go to the residence of Pete Maxwell, a man who up to that time I had never seen...." [63]

If Poe is correct, it shows Garrett's evident reluctance to pursue Billy at Fort Sumner.

"Garrett then proposed that we go into a grove of trees near the town, conceal our horses, then station ourselves in the peach orchard at the rear of [Pete's] house, and keep watch on who might come or go." [64]

It was about 9 o'clock at night when the three men sneaked into Fort Sumner:

"We approached these houses cautiously, and when within ear shot, heard the sound of voices conversing in Spanish. We concealed ourselves quickly and listened; but the distance was too great to hear words, or even distinguish voices. Soon a man arose from the ground, in full view, but too far away to recognize.... With a few words, which fell like a murmur on our ears, he went to the fence, jumped it, and walked down toward Maxwell's house." [65]

Neither Poe nor McKinney had ever met Billy, so only Garrett was capable of identifying their target. The reason for the two deputies being present was simple – if Billy was found, Garrett expected a gunfight, and he wanted the odds weighed heavily in his favor.

After watching for about two hours, and seeing no indication of Billy, the three men approached the large, 12-room, adobe structure where Pete Maxwell, his mother, his sister Paulita, and other family members were living. The original purpose of the building, when the Fort was under military control, was as officers' quarters. Pete's room was in the southeastern corner of the building. The door to his room opened onto a porch, which was fronted by a white picket fence.

"This is Maxwell's room in the corner. You fellows wait here while I go in and talk to him." [66]

In response to these instructions of Garrett's, Poe crouched on the edge of the porch and McKinney squatted on his heels just outside the fence.[67]

Garrett slipped soundlessly into Pete's room – the door was wide open:

"...on account of the extremely warm weather." [68]

"There were three windows in the room, all of which were raised. Through the open door and windows the moonlight streamed into the room." [69]

Inside the room, Garrett saw Pete *"lying on the bed in the S. E. corner of the room."* Garrett sat on the edge of the bed, positioning himself so he *"was able to partially hide himself in the shadow."* [70]

> *"I... had just commenced talking to [Pete] about the object of my visit at such an unusual hour, when a man entered the room in stockinged feet, with a pistol in one hand and a knife in the other."* [71]

Outside, just seconds earlier, Poe had been startled by the stealthy approach of that same mysterious figure:

> *"...my attention was attracted, from where I sat in the little gateway, to a man approaching me on the inside of and along the fence, some forty or fifty steps away. I observed that he was only partially dressed and was both bare-headed and barefooted, or rather, had only socks on his feet, and it seemed to me that he was fastening his trousers as he came toward me at a brisk walk."* [72]

> *"Upon seeing me, he covered me with his six-shooter as quick as lightning, sprang onto the porch, calling out in Spanish 'Quien es?' – at the same time backing away from me toward the door through which Garrett only a few seconds before had passed, repeating his query, 'Who is it?' in Spanish several times."* [73]

In Pete's room, Garrett squinted at the silhouette in the doorway, starkly outlined by the moon, its features obscured in shadow:

> *"He came and placed his hand on the bed just beside me, and in a low whisper [asked], 'who is it?'"*

> *"I at once recognized the man [from his voice], and knew he was the Kid, and reached behind me for my pistol, feeling almost certain of receiving a ball from his at the moment of doing so, as I felt sure he had now recognized me, but fortunately he drew back from the bed at noticing my movement, and although he had his pistol pointed at my breast, he delayed to fire, and asked in Spanish, 'Quien es? Quein es?' This gave me time to bring mine to bear on him, and the moment I did so I pulled the trigger and he received his death wound, for the ball struck him in the left breast and pierced his heart."* [74]

Garrett fired a second time before he could see the effect of the first shot, but that shot missed its intended target, striking the room wall and glancing *"off the headboard of a wooden bedstead."* [75]

Outside, Poe:

> *"...heard a groan and one or two gasps... as of someone dying in the room. An instant later, Garrett came out, brushing against me as he passed. He stood by me close to the wall at the side of the door and said to me, 'That was the Kid that came in there onto me, and I think I have got him.' I said, 'Pat, the Kid would not come to this place; you have shot the wrong man."* [76]

Garrett replied:

> *"I am sure that was him, as I know his voice too well to be mistaken."* [77]

Pete, panic-stricken, had bolted out of the room on Garrett's heels, dragging *"his bedclothes with him."* [78]

Garrett's shots roused the members of the Maxwell household, who rapidly gathered outside Pete's room. Those present included Pete's mother Luz Maxwell, Pete's sisters Paulita and Odila Maxwell, Deluvina Maxwell, Pete's uncle Pablo Beaubien and his wife Rebecca, and Pablo Abreu. They were quickly joined by many others, including A. P. "Paco" Anaya, Higinio Garcia, Jesus Silva, Sabal and Celsa Guiterrez, Martin and Abrana Garcia, Lorenzo and Jose Jaramillo, Vincente Otero, Isaac Sandoval, Frank Lobato, Marie Lobato, and George Miller (a black soldier who was spending the night at Fort Sumner). [79]

No one in the crowd stepped forward to look inside Pete's room for fear that Billy was still alive and would shoot the first person he saw. Finally, someone produced a lit lamp – many sources say it was Deluvina Maxwell – which was placed on the ledge of one of the open windows.[80]

The light revealed Billy on the floor, on his back – *"a six-shooter lying at his right hand and a butcher knife at his left."* [81]

Initially, Poe and McKinney thought that Billy had fired once before he died, as they believed they had heard a third shot. On inspecting Billy's six-shooter, Garrett found that it was:

> *"...a self-cocker, calibre .41. It had five cartridges and one shell in the chambers, the hammer resting on the shell, but this proves nothing, as many carry their revolvers in this way for safety; besides, this shell looked as though it had been shot some time before."* [82]

Fateful Choice

So why did Billy walk into his death, in Pete's room?

In describing his entrance into Fort Sumner, Garrett wrote:

> *"Soon a man arose from the ground, in full view, but too far away to recognize...."* [83]

He later made the subject of his statement clear:

> *"Little as we suspected it, this man was the Kid."* [84]

Garrett was implying that Billy had been sleeping with his girlfriend in the orchard.

Reporting what he learned after the killing, Garrett wrote that after leaving the orchard, Billy:

> *"...went to the house of a Mexican friend, pulled off his hat and boots, threw himself on a bed, and commenced reading a newspaper. He soon, however, hailed his friend, who was sleeping in the room, told him to get up and make some coffee, adding – 'Give me a butcher knife, and I will go over to Pete's and get some beef; I'm hungry.'"* [85]

Garrett does not name the *"friend,"* but by adding that he was asleep, he suggests that the friend was the unwitting husband of Billy's girlfriend.

Paco Anaya, who was present at the killing, and knew Billy well, gives a different account. He says that Billy was visiting the home of Jesus Silva, where Anaya spoke with him. Early in the evening of July 14, Billy and Silva left to water a horse that Billy had hidden at a nearby ranch. On returning to Fort Sumner, Billy went to the home of Sabal and Celsa Gutierrez, where Billy was staying.[86]

Then, quoting Celsa Gutierrez, Anaya writes:

> *"Billy entered the house, and he was carrying a bone. This was the hock of a leg, and when he had come in, he went straight to the kitchen, and returning to the room where we were, me and Sabal, Billy said to me, 'Celsa, I brought you some meat for you to make my supper.'"* [87]

On checking the *"bone,"* Celsa decided it was not worth cooking.

Billy then got a butcher knife and left the Gutierrez house, intending to cut some meat off a side of beef that was hanging on Pete's porch.[88]

A third, contemporaneous account, says:

> *"[Billy] had gone at once to the house of Manuella Bowdre, [the wife] of one of Billy's old compadres, Charlie Bowdre, who was shot when 'the Kid,' Rudabaugh, Tom Pickett and Billy Wilson were 'rounded up' at Stinking Springs...."* [89]

The same account also notes:

> *"Since his escape, [Billy] had allowed his beard to grow and had attempted to disguise himself as a Mexican by darkening his skin by the use of some sort of root."* [90]

A fourth account, based on stories told by descendents of Abrana (Segura) Garcia, says that Billy had spent the evening with Abrana, prior to crossing to the Maxwell house to obtain some meat for supper. This is the sole account that embraces a specific a person as Billy's girlfriend.[91]

All four accounts make it clear that Billy was among staunch friends, who certainly would have warned him if they had even the slightest suspicion of danger close by.

So Billy's fateful choice to visit the Maxwell house, at the fateful moment that Garrett was in Pete's room, set up his death.

And then when Billy chose to ask "Quien es?" rather than retreat or shoot, he cinched his death.

If Garrett had encountered Billy in any other way, the result would certainly have been a gunfight – and the consequence – unpredictable. Garrett recognized this:

> *"I went out contemplating the probability of being shot at, and the possibility of being hurt, perhaps killed; but not if any precaution on my part would prevent such a catastrophe...."*

> *"Then, the 'lucky shot,' as they put it. It was not the shot, but the opportunity that was lucky, and everybody may rest assured I did not hesitate long to improve it."* [92]

18 ~ Chapter 1

Justifiable Homicide

Once it was apparent that Billy was dead, Garrett re-entered the room:

"...and examined the body. The ball struck him just above the heart, and must have cut through the ventricles." [93]

The news of Billy's death was not received well by the large crowd gathered outside at Maxwell's, as Poe noted:

"[Garrett, McKinney, and I were] keeping constantly on our guard, as we were expecting to be attacked by the friends of the dead man." [94]

Jesus Silva, with the help of others, lifted the body and took it into a hallway of the Maxwell house, and laid it on a long table. There, a thorough examination confirmed Billy was dead:

"Strange as it may seem, that wound did not bleed for two hours after he was shot." [95]

The body was then moved to a bench in a nearby blacksmith/carpenter shop.[96]

The Justice of Peace for Fort Sumner, Alejandro Segura, was sent for. He lived in Arenosa, a tiny settlement about seven miles away. When Segura arrived, he convened a coroner's jury consisting of Milnor Rudulph, Antonio Saavedra, Pedro Antonio Lucero, Jose Silva, Sabal Gutierrez, and Lorenzo Jaramillo – who all knew Billy well.[97]

The coroner's jury report, written in Spanish, quoted the following evidence, supplied by Pete Maxwell:

"As I was lying down on my bed in my room about midnight the fourteenth (14th) of July, Pat F. Garrett entered my room and sat down on the edge of my bed to talk to me. Shortly after Garrett had sat down, Wm. Bonney entered and came over to my bed with a pistol in his hand and asked me 'Who is it? Who is it?' And then Pat F. Garrett shot two bullets at said William Bonney and the said Wm. Bonney fell to one side of my stove and I left the room. When I entered again 3 or 4 minutes after the shots, said Bonney was dead." [98] *(English translation)*

The jury then ruled:

"We of the jury unanimously find that Wm. Bonny has been killed by a bullet, fired from the pistol in the hand of Pat F. Garrett, in the left breast in the region of the heart, and our decision is that the deed of said Garrett, was justifiable homicide and we are unanimous in the opinion that the gratitude of the whole community is owed to said Garrett for his deed and that he is worthy of being rewarded." [99] *(English translation)*

Dead or Alive

On April 30, 1881, Governor Wallace had issued a $500 reward *"to any person or persons who will capture William Bonny, alias the Kid, and deliver him to any sheriff of New Mexico."* [100] "Capture" obviously meant alive, but it was understood by all that the reward was for Billy dead or alive.

Five days after Billy's killing, Garrett was in Santa Fe, New Mexico, to collect the reward:

"Yesterday afternoon Pat Garrett, accompanied by Hon. T. B. Catron and Col. M. Brunswick, called upon acting-Governor Ritch in regard to the reward offered by ex-Governor Lew Wallace for the Kid. The reward was fixed at five hundred dollars and the offer was published in the papers. Governor Ritch announced that he was willing to pay the amount, and would be glad to do so, but that he would have to look over the records first. He was not in the city when the offer was made, and had never received any notification of it, consequently did not know whether or not it was on record. In consequence of this state of affairs, the question of the reward was not settled." [101]

Acting Governor William G. Ritch had replaced Governor Wallace on May 30, 1881.

After three days consideration, Governor Ritch decided that Wallace's offer of a reward was not legal, and refused to pay.

But public sentiment strongly supported rewarding Garrett. The White Oaks' *Golden Era* editor put it this way:

"It is not enough to be thankful and offer our sheriff congratulations only, we must give a stronger recognition. He must be amply rewarded. We must stand by our officers who do their duties so nobly, at such a great expense and at such great risks. Let every one subscribe and pay freely for this brave and commendable act, that Mr. Garrett may not only know that his services are appreciated, but that for them he is entitled to be rewarded in a monetary sense." [102]

The first person to start a collection for Garrett was James Dolan, Billy's deeply despised, murderous enemy during the Lincoln County War:

"Early yesterday morning Mr. James Dolan, one of the Lincoln county men with reason for congratulation upon the death of the Kid, started out with a subscription list in search of donations to the fund to be presented to Pat F. Garrett, sheriff of Lincoln county, and the slayer of the worst man the territory has known. Two men who are interested in property in the South headed the list with subscriptions of one hundred dollars each. These were followed by donations ranging from twenty-five dollars down, and before night the sum had reached five hundred sixty dollars. The list was carried around in the afternoon and was also successful in securing subscriptions. It is hoped by those who have the matter in hand that the sum will be raised to at least six hundred dollars. Garrett deserves every cent of this and more, but if the other towns do as well he will receive a good round sum." [103]

In Mesilla, the editor of *Thirty-Four* started a Garrett fund that collected more than $250.[104]

In Las Vegas:

"When the news of the killing of 'Billy the Kid' was brought to the city it was decided that Garrett should be handsomely remunerated for his trouble,

and when THE OPTIC urged the same thing last night the matter was as good as settled. A fund was started and has reached nearly $1,000 already." [105]

This fund eventually reached more than $1,300.[106]

"Santa Fe will probably beat Las Vegas, although people, as a rule, are not subscribing as liberally as they should. There are some exceptions to this rule, of course, as some of the contributions were very handsome." [107]

A year and two days after Billy's killing, Garrett finally got the $500 promised by Governor Wallace. On July 18, 1882, the New Mexico Territorial Legislature passed a special act authorizing the payment of Garrett's reward:

"An Act For the Relief of Pat Garrett"

"The Territorial Auditor is hereby authorized to draw a warrant upon the Territorial Treasury of the Territory of New Mexico in favor of Pat Garrett for the sum of Five Hundred Dollars payable out of any funds in the Territorial Treasury." [108]

Between the collections and the legislative authorization, Garrett received as much as $7,000 in reward money.[109] He was also given a gold sheriff's badge in the shape of a star. The front of the badge reads:

Lincoln County
Sheriff

The back of the badge reads:

To Pat Garrett
With Best Regards of
A. J. Fountain
1881 [110]

Attorney Albert J. Fountain had unsuccessfully defended Billy in his trial for the murder of Sheriff William Brady. That he rewarded Billy's killer with a gold badge undoubtedly revealed his attitude toward Billy's killing of Bell and Olinger. It may or may not have reflected his attitude toward Billy's conviction for killing Brady.

Poe and McKinney also received reward money, although the sources and amounts are unknown. It may be that Garrett shared a portion of his reward with his deputies.[111]

Press Response

Billy's death was reported in the national press, from California to New York, in over fifty newspapers. Even the *London Times* published a lengthy notice of his death.[112] The editorial tone of the newspaper coverage was predominantly celebratory, as in the following report by the Silver City newspaper:

"The vulgar murderer and desperado known as 'Billy the Kid' has met his just deserts at last.... Despite the glamour of romance thrown around his dare-devil life by sensational writers, the fact is he was a low down vulgar cut-throat, with probably not one redeeming quality." [113]

The *Santa Fe Weekly Democrat* sneered:

"He is dead; and he died so suddenly that he did not have time to be interviewed by a preacher, or to sing hymns, or pray, so we cannot say positively that he has clumb the shining ladder and entered the pearly gates...."

"No sooner had the floor caught his descending form, which had a pistol in one hand and a knife in the other, than there was a strong order of brimstone in the air, and a dark figure, with the wings of a dragon, claws like a tiger, eyes like balls of fire and horns like a bison, hovered over the corpse for a moment, and with a fiendish laugh said, 'Ha, ha, this is my meat' and sailed off through a window." [114]

The *Las Vegas Daily Optic* thanked God and invoked vampires:

"A glorious God-send – the killing of 'the Kid.'"

"If Pat Garrett is not paid a couple of thousand dollars for ridding the county of its worst vampire – 'Billy, the Kid' – the people are simply n. g. [no good]" [115]

The White Oaks *Lincoln County Leader* made the following compelling observation:

"'The trouble with Bill was he talked before he shot. Always before that he shot first and talked afterward. That's the testimony of Pete Maxwell, eyewitness to the killing of William H. Bonney, known far and wide in the territory as Billy, The Kid.'" [116]

The *Leader* was one of the few papers that had anything decent to say about Billy:

"Padre Redin at Anton Chico says, 'Billy did not have a bad heart, really. Most of his crimes were crimes of vengeance.'" [117]

"The Authentic Life of Billy the Kid"

Five months after Billy's death, the Mesilla newspaper revealed:

"Sheriff Pat Garrett of Lincoln Co. has closed a contract with the New Mexican Publishing Co. of Santa Fe for the publication of the Live [Life] of Billy the Kid. The book will contain 128 pages and will be sold at 50 cents a copy." [118]

Garrett's book, titled *"The Authentic Life of Billy, the Kid, the Noted Desperado of the Southwest, Whose Deeds of Daring Have Made His Name a Terror in New Mexico, Arizona, and Northern Mexico,"* appeared April 1, 1882. The Mesilla newspaper favorably reviewed the book:

"The 'Life of Billy the Kid' by Pat Garrett of Lincoln is before us. It is well printed, and handsomely illustrated. As we were looking over it, two or three men from Lincoln dropped in, and at once took up the book and looked at the pictures. All of them knew 'the Kid' well, and had seen and spoken to him often. They pronounced the portraits good likenesses; and on glancing over the

22 ~ Chapter 1

reading matter, Mr. Burt, the postmaster of Lincoln, came across an account of 'the Kid's escaping with his (Burt's) horse. He said the description of the affair was accurate in every particular, and then he sat down to devour the whole contents of the volume. On returning the book he remarked that, on the whole, the story was well and truthfully rendered, and decidedly interesting." [119]

The Mesilla newspaper further noted:

"The book is selling very fast in this city. Nearly every 'old residenter' has purchased one. Our own copy has already been borrowed a dozen times, at least." [120]

But not all reviews were good. The Las Vegas *Daily Optic* opined:

"Pat Garrett is sick at Roswell. Probably the 'Life of Billy the Kid' in print as executed by the New Mexican gave him gangrene of the bowels." [121]

The book did not sell well because the small Santa Fe publisher picked by Garrett had no national distribution. If Garrett's book had been published by one of the major New York publishers, undoubtedly the book would have sold many thousands of copies, as did several bogus accounts of Billy's life that were published shortly after his death.

Photos

Territory of New Mexico Third Judicial District Judge Warren Henry Bristol. On April 14, 1881, Judge Bristol sentenced Billy the Kid to *"be hanged by the neck until his body be dead."*

Proclamation by the Governor.

For the information of the people of the United States, and of the citizens of New Mexico in especial, the undersigned announces that the disorders lately prevalent in Lincoln County in said Territory, have been happily brought to an end. Persons having business and property interests therein, and who are themselves peaceably disposed, may go to and from that County without hinderance or molestation. Individuals resident there, but who have been driven away, or who, from choice, sought safety elsewhere, are invited to return, under assurance that ample measures have been taken, and are now and will be continued in force, to make them secure in person and property. And that the people of Lincoln County may be helped more speedily to the management of their civil affairs, as contemplated by law, and to induce them to lay aside forever the divisions and feuds which, by national no oriety, have been so prejudicial to their locality and the whole Territory, the undersigned, by virtue of authority in him vested, further proclaims a general pardon for misdemeanors and offenses committed in the said County of Lincoln against the laws of the said Territory in connection with the aforesaid disorders, between the first day of February, 1878, and the date of this proclamation.

And it is expressly understood that the foregoing pardon is upon the conditions and limitations following:

It shall not apply except to officers of the United States Army stationed in the said County during the said disorders, and to persons who, at the time of the commission of the offense or misdemeanor of which they may be accused, were, with good intent, resident citizens of the said Territory, and who shall have hereafter kept the peace, and conducted themselves in all respects as becomes good citizens.

Neither shall it be pleaded by any person in bar of conviction under indictment now found and returned for any such crimes or misdemeanors, nor operate the release of any party undergoing pains and penalties consequent upon sentence heretofore had for any crime or misdemeanor.

In witness whereof I have hereunto set may hand and caused the seal of the Territory of New Mexico to be affixed.

{ SEAL. } Done at the city of Santa Fé, this 13th day of November, A D. 1878.
LEWIS WALLACE,

By the Governor,
W. G. RITCH,
Secretary.

Para la informacion del pueblo de los Estados Unidos, y de los ciudadanos del Territorio de Nuevo Mojico en lo especial, el abajo firmado anuncia que los desórdenes que hace poco tiempo predominaban en el Condado de Lincoln, en dicho Territorio, han llegado felizmente á su fin. Personas que tengan negocios y propiedad é intereses en él mismo, y que están pacificamente dispuestas pueden entrar y salir de ese condado sin obstaculo ni vejacion. Individuos residentes alli, pero que han sido impelidos á salir, ó que por escojimiento han buscado seguridad en otras partes, son invitadas de regresar, bajo la seguridad que se han tomado medidas amplias y están ahora y serán continuadas en fuerza, para asegurarles en su propiedad.

Y para que el pueblo del condado de Lincoln sea mas prontamente ayudado en el manejo de sus asuntos locales como contemplado por la ley, y para inducirles de dejar á un lado y para siempre las divisiones y disensiones, que por notoriedad nacional han sido tan perjudiciales á su localidad y á todo el Territorio, el abajo firmado, por virtud de autoridad en el investida, ademas proclama un perdon general por malos procederes y ofensas cometidas en el dicho condado de Lincoln contra las leyes del dicho territorio, en concecion con los arriba dichos desórdenes, entre el dia primero de Febrero mil ochocientos setenta y ocho y la fecha de esta proclamacion.

Y es expresamente entendido que el perdon arriba dicho es sobre las condiciones y limitaciones siguientes: No se aplicará excepto á oficiales del Ejercito de los Estados Unidos apostados en dicho condado durante los dichos desórdenes, y á personas que, al tiempo de cometer la ofensa ó mal proceder de la cual puedan ser acusados, eran con buena intencion ciudadanos residentes de dicho territorio, y quienes en lo de adelante guarden la paz y se conduscan en todos respectos como conviene á ciudadanos buenos. Ni tampoco se alegará por ninguna persona en foro de conviccion bajo querella ahora hallada y retornada por cualesquier tales crimenes ó malos procederes, ni obrará la exoneracion de ninguna parte sufriendo castigos y penas consecuentes sobre sentencia dada antes por ningun crímen ó mal proceder.

En testimonio de lo cual he puesto á esta mi mano, y he causado que sea fijado el sello del Territorio de Nuevo Mejico.

{ SELLO } Hecha en la ciudad de Santa Fé, este dia 13 de Noviembre, A. D., 1878,
LEWIS WALLACE,

Por el Gobernador:
W. G. RITCH, Secretario.

Pardon issued by Territorial Governor Lewis "Lew" Wallace, November 13, 1878.
Courtesy Lew Wallace Collection, Indiana State Historical Society.

Sheriff Patrick F. Garrett. Photo taken in the early 1880s. Courtesy Maurice G. Fulton Papers, Special Collections, UA.

26 ~ Chapter 1

Mesilla Courthouse – Built 1865 – Site of Billy the Kid's Trial - About 1885. Courtesy Joe Lopez.

Mesilla Courthouse – Today.

28 ~ Chapter 1

Lincoln County Courthouse, about 1930.

Killing Billy – "Kid Talked Before He Shot" ~ 29

Lincoln County Courthouse, 1952. The white "x" marks the window from which Billy shot Deputy Marshal Robert Olinger.

Gottfried Gauss, eye-witness to Billy's escape from the Lincoln County Courthouse. Undated photograph. Courtesy Courtesy Archives and Special Collections, NMSU.

Yginio Salazar. Billy's first stop after escaping from the Lincoln County Courthouse was at Salazar's place to get his shackles cut off. Undated photograph. Courtesy Maurice G. Fulton Papers, Special Collections, UA.

Deluvina Maxwell at her home at Fort Sumner a few years before her death. Girl unidentified. Courtesy Center for Southwest Research and Special Collections, UNM.

Deputy Sheriff John William Poe. Undated photo. Courtesy Maurice G. Fulton Papers, Special Collections, UA.

Maxwell residence at Fort Sumner. Formerly the officers' quarters for the fort. Pete Maxwell's room was in the front, left (southeast) corner. The visible figures are Maxwell family members.

Lucien Bonaparte Maxwell. Lucien bought the Fort Sumner grounds and buildings on October, 17, 1870, for $5,000. Undated photo. Courtesy Arthur Johnson Memorial Library.

Seated: Peter "Pete" Menard Maxwell. Standing: Henry Leis. Undated photo.
Courtesy Arthur Johnson Memorial Library.

Paulita "Paula" Maxwell and José Francisco Jaramillo, wedding photo, January 14, 1882. Paula wrote Billy while he was in the Mesilla jail, and is the most likely candidate for Billy's girlfriend. Courtesy Arthur Johnson Memorial Library.

Milnor Rudulph. Rudulph served on the coroner's jury that ruled Billy's death "justifiable homicide." Photo taken in the mid-1880's. Courtesy Archives and Special Collections, NMSU.

The gold badge given to Sheriff Patrick F. Garrett by Colonel Albert J. Fountain as a reward for killing Billy the Kid. Photo courtesy of Lori Ann Goodloe.

Cover of Sheriff Pat Garrett's book on Billy the Kid, published by the New Mexican Printing and Publishing Co. of Santa Fe, April 1, 1882.

Chapter 2 | Billy's Grave - "The Bivouac of the Dead"

In 1862, when Fort Sumner was established, a lot roughly one-half of an acre was set aside as a cemetery.

Between 1862 and 1868, there were 22 military burials in the Fort Sumner cemetery, 21 soldiers and one civilian. The civilian was killed resisting military arrest. It is possible, even likely, that additional civilians were buried in the cemetery during these years, although no records of such burials exist. On March 20, 1867, Lieutenant Robert M. McDonald, after visiting Fort Sumner, wrote:

> *"[The cemetery] is now enclosed by a wall of adobes five feet high and twenty-seven inches wide at the bottom, sloping to a point at the top. Trees have been planted throughout, the Graves are in good condition, Head Boards placed at each & every grave. The sodding of graves is impracticable in this locality as the grasses are of that peculiar kind that will not grow thick enough."* [1]

Following the purchase of Fort Sumner by Lucian Maxwell in 1870, the cemetery became the accepted burial place for Fort Sumner residents.

Billy's Burial

Early in the morning of July 15, 1881, the coroner's jury met over Billy's body in the blacksmith/carpenter shop. As noted, the jury's ruling was that Billy had been killed by Sheriff Pat Garrett with a bullet to the left breast and the killing was *"justifiable homicide."* [2]

The body was then prepared for burial by Deluvina Maxwell. Billy was dressed in:

> *"...a beige suit, a shirt, an undershirt, shorts, and a pair of stockings."* [3]

Garrett paid for the clothes.[4]

Jesus Silva recounted what happened next:

> *"...at 10 o'clock we buried Billy the Kid in the little cemetery near the old Fort, beside the bodies of Billy's former pals, Charlie Bowdre and Tom O'Folliard, who were killed by officers earlier."*

> *"I was chief pallbearer at Billy's funeral that morning. With me were Antonio Savadera, Saval Gutierez [Sabal Gutierrez], Vincente Otero and a few others. We buried the Kid in a grave which had been dug by Vincente Otero."* [5]

Almost everyone who lived in Fort Sumner attended Billy's funeral. [6]

> *"The day after the funeral Pete Maxwell had his man pull a wooden picket from the parade-ground fence, saw off a foot or so, and nail it in a crossbar to the longer piece. Then he printed in crude letters BILLY THE KID, JULY 14, 1881."* [7]

Shortly after the hastily-made, wooden-picket marker was placed over Billy's grave, it was riddled with bullet holes, fired by a party of drunken soldiers. [8]

42 ~ Chapter 2

The Cost of Fame

Ten days after Billy's burial, the *Las Vegas Daily Optic* dropped a bombshell on its readers:

"The Fatal Finger"

"An esteemed friend of THE OPTIC at Fort Sumner, L. W. Hale, has sent us the index finger of 'Billy, the Kid,' the one which has snapped many a man's life into eternity. It is well-preserved in alcohol and has been viewed by many in our office to-day. If the rush continues we shall purchase a small tent and open a side show to which complimentary tickets will be issued to our personal friends." [9]

This was followed by an even more nauseating claim:

"Scarcely has the news of the killing of William Bonney, alias McCarthy, but known the wide-world over as 'Billy, the Kid,' faded from the public mind before we are again to be startled by the second chapter in the bloody romance of his eventful life – the disposal of his body."

"The fifth day after the burial of the notorious young desperado, a fearless skelologist of this county, whose name for substantial reasons, cannot be divulged"

"PROCEEDED TO SUMNER,"

"and in the silent watches of the night, with the assistance of a compadre, dug up the remains of the once mighty youth and carried them off in a wagon."

"The 'stiff' was brought to Las Vegas, arriving here at two o'clock in the morning, and was slipped quietly into the private office of a practical 'sawbones,' who, by dint of diligent labor and careful watching to prevent detection, boiled and scraped the skin off the 'pate' so as to secure"

"THE SKULL"

"which was seen by a reporter last evening. The body, or remains proper, was covered in the dirt in the corral where it will remain until decomposition shall have robbed the frame of the meat, when the body will be dug up again and the skeleton 'fixed up' – hung together by wires and varnished with shelac [shellac] to make it presentable."

"The index finger of the right hand, it will be remembered, was presented to THE OPTIC at the time the exhumation was made. As this member has been sent east, the skeleton now in process of consummation will not be complete in its fingers; but the loss is so trivial that it will hardly be noticeable." [10]

The editor of the *Daily Optic* achieved his goal: the news of Billy's grave robbery and skull-skinning was picked up and reprinted in numerous newspapers across the country.

Aware that once the lurid sensationalism had died down, the editor – having added his personal testimony to the story – knew he would be pressed for believable confirmation of what he had reported. He justified his inability to do so by conveniently claiming he no longer had the evidence:

"Billy, the Kid, had a sweetheart, so we have just learned. The young lady's name is Kate Tenney and she lives on Fifteenth street in Oakland, California. She read in the newspapers that THE OPTIC had the index finger of the Kid in pickle, and she has written for it, with a request to send also a photograph of the young killer. We have written Miss Tenney a sorrowful epistle, full of touching condolence and broke the news gently that we had just sold our relic of her lover for $150 cash, and that 'Billy' was such a contrary fellow that he wouldn't sit still long enough for a photographer to get his camera turned loose upon him, hence the photograph she craved must ever be forthcoming. We will see that physician who was fortunate enough to secure Billy's 'stiff' and will present a request for some part of the Kid's skeleton – a shank bone, or something of that kind, which we will send to the broken-hearted maiden as a lasting memento of her dead lover's former greatness." [11]

The *Daily Optic's* final mention of this event was three months after Billy's death:

"At last accounts THE OPTIC's preserved finger of Billy, the Kid, 'the mysterious member,' as Sergeant Hardy would call it, was in Indiana on exhibition at the county fairs. THE OPTIC generally has a finger in every pie that's going." [12]

Sheriff Garrett was disgusted by the *Daily Optic's* grisly claims:

"I said that the body was buried in the cemetery at Fort Sumner; I wish to add that it is there to-day intact – skull, fingers, toes, bones, and every hair of the head that was buried with the body on that 15th day of July, doctors, newspaper editors, and paragraphers to the contrary notwithstanding."

"Some presuming swindlers have claimed to have the Kid's skull on exhibition, or one of his fingers, or some other portion of his body, and one medical gentleman has persuaded credulous idiots that he has all the bones strung upon wires...."

"Again I say that the Kid's body lies undisturbed in the grave, and I speak of what I know." [13]

Poe was equally appalled:

"The story that we had cut off and carried away his fingers was even more absurd, as the thought of such never entered our minds, and beside we were not that kind of people." [14]

That the finger story was a fraud was revealed by a letter to the *Daily Optic* ten years after the original *Daily Optic* story:

"Those Bones Being Fetched In"

"Never fool a professional man, because, being a humbug himself, he never forgives being humbugged. If any one ever said this before, I don't know it but it goes without saying."

44 ~ Chapter 2

"I admit participation in the 'Billy the Kid' finger fraud, but the scheme originated in the fertile brain of our now worthy county clerk. The editor of the Optic remarked that he would get even, but he is away off on the bones...."

"Yours truly,"
"Frank N. Page" [15]

Paulita's Midnight Visit

Shortly after Billy's funeral, Paulita Maxwell was visiting with her brother Pete and her brother-in-law Manuel Abreu. It was late in the evening and the conversation turned to Billy:

"The town and house were silent. Suddenly we heard a strange noise like softly padding footsteps. It gave us all a thrill. The Kid had been killed in an adjoining bedroom. The sound was ghostly. It ceased. It began again. Just like someone walking softly in stockinged feet." [16]

Pete said he had heard these queer noises before, suggesting it was Billy's ghost. Paulita laughed, saying she had no patience with people who believed in ghosts. She was challenged to prove it by visiting Billy's grave. After initially declining, she agreed, and left for the cemetery. It was nearly midnight. After a long wait she returned, bringing the rough cross that had been placed over Billy's grave.

The cross was returned to the cemetery the next morning.[17]

The First Tourist

In January, 1882, six months after Billy's death, the *Daily Optic* printed the account of a curious visitor to the Fort Sumner cemetery:

"THE BIVOUAC OF THE DEAD"

"A Visit to an Old Burying Ground at Fort Sumner"

"Special Correspondence of The Optic"

"To the southwest of the abandoned and decaying Fort Sumner lies the graveyard, surrounded by what was once a good adobe wall, but from decay and neglect is now merely an outline, surrounding an acre of ground. We enter on the north, walking over the remains of the once handsome gate. To the left, in the northeast corner, are the graves of four rustlers – Grant, killed by Billy, the Kid; Ferris [Farris], who was killed by Barney Mason at the insistence of the Kid, and O'Fallion [O'Folliard] and Bowdre, who were killed by Pat Garrett and posse. These graves are all unmarked, and that of Bowdre shows the scratching of some hungry coyote, who seems to have been scared away by something before he reached his prey."

"To the right of the entrance lies the grave of Billy the Kid, marked by a plain board, with the stenciled letters:"

```
|"BILLY |
| THE   |
| KID"  |
```

"It snowed last night, and the only marks on the grave were the tracks of a rabbit or skunk."

"The southwest part of the little burying ground is filled with graves of soldiers who were killed in a fight with Indians near the fort as the few legible headboards read, 'July 7, 1866.'"

"Over in the southwest corner lies the grave of Lucien B. Maxwell, once so famous in New Mexico."

"This 'silent city of the dead' this morning, with the snow covering the graves, looks dreary, deserted and neglected, and we think, as we look at the white mounds, that the brave soldiers who fell fighting doing their duty, would spurn the company of the rustlers from their silent bivouac." [18]

Fort Sumner Abandoned

On January 15, 1884, Luz and Pete Maxwell sold most of the family's extensive land holdings, including Fort Sumner, to four buyers who formed the Fort Sumner Cattle & Land Company. Luz then homesteaded 160 acres several miles south of the Fort, taking with her Pete and other family members.[19] The new owners of the Fort required the residents then living at the site to leave also, which led to the Fort's abandonment as a settlement.[20] In 1891, a visitor noted:

"[The] old place is in ruins. At one time, the officer's quarters were fine, the residences well-fitted up for comfort, but now one boarding house only, kept by W. S. Chadderdon. It is not first-class in anything but prices." [21]

On June 21, 1898, Pete Maxwell quietly died at Luz's home, aged 50. He was buried in the Fort Sumner cemetery the following day.[22]

Billy's Grave Misplaced in Public Imagination

In the two decades following Billy's death, newspapers continued to print stories about Billy the Kid, but knowledge of where Billy was buried dropped from public consciousness.

In 1901, Emerson Hough, a hugely popular Western writer, wrote:

"Today Pat Garrett, prosperous ranchman, quiet, gentle, and singularly reticent regarding anything having to do with Billy the Kid, lives at Las Cruces, in the far southwest. Near him is the grave of Billy the Kid, one of the worst outlaws of the west, and certainly bad as man could be." [23]

Hough's mistaken placing of Billy's grave in Las Cruces is particularly surprising given that Hough had moved to White Oaks, New Mexico, in December, 1882, just months after Billy's death. He would correct this mistake four years later.

The idea that Billy was buried in Las Cruces was repeated by the press numerous times. For example, an interview with ex-New Mexico territorial governor Lew Wallace reported:

"To-day there is a little lowly heap of earth located at Las Cruces, N. M. To the curious stranger some idle native may, now and again, point out this little

46 ~ Chapter 2

grave and explain, with a certain pride, that Las Cruces possesses the final resting place of the worst man that ever infested the southwestern border." [24]

This is just one example of the many false facts that were current at the time in stories about Billy the Kid.

Cemetery Flooded

On October 8, 1904, following almost two weeks of record-breaking rains, the Pecos River burst its banks and flooded Fort Sumner and the surrounding area.[25] The flood crested seven feet above the Pecos River banks. Water stood on top of the Fort Sumner cemetery four feet deep for over a week.[26]

Some writers have suggested that this once-in-a-century flood washed out Billy's grave. This is doubtful, as will be seen.

Garrett Revisits Billy's Grave

In early October, 1905, Emerson Hough sought out Pat Garrett to interview him for an article on Billy the Kid. The two men became good friends, and Garrett agreed to take Hough on a personal tour of sites in New Mexico associated with Billy and other New Mexican gunmen.[27]

On October 14, 1905, Garrett and Hough left El Paso, Texas, by horse-drawn wagon. They planned to feed themselves by hunting and fishing, and to spend the nights camping wherever *"night overtook them."* [28]

On October 25, 1905, Garrett and Hough reached Fort Sumner:

"...old Fort Sumner, once a famous military post..., offered nothing better than a scene of desolation, there being no longer a single human inhabitant there. The old avenue of cottonwoods, once four miles long, is now ragged and unwatered, and the great parade ground has gone back to sand and sage brush. We were obliged to search for some time before we could find the site of the Maxwell house, in which was enacted the last tragedy in the life of a once famous bad man. Garrett finally located the spot, now only a rough quadrangle of crumbled earthen walls."

"'This is the place,' said he, pointing at one corner of the grass-grown oblong. 'Pete Maxwell's bed was right in this corner of the room and I was sitting in the dark and talking to Pete, who was in bed. The Kid passed John Poe and Tip McKinney, my deputies, right over there on what was then the gallery, and came through the door right here.'"

"Twenty-five years of time had done their work in all that country, as we learned when we entered the little barbed-wire enclosure of the cemetery where the Kid and his fellows were buried. There are no headstones in this cemetery, and no sacristan holds its records. Again Garrett had to search in the salt grass and greasewood. 'Here is the place,' said he at length. 'We buried them all in a row. The first grave is the Kid's, and the next to him is Bowdre, and then O'Folliard. There's nothing left to mark them.'"

"So passes the glory of this world. Even the headboard which once stood at the Kid's grave – and which was once riddled with bullets by cowards who would not have dared to shoot that close to him had he been alive – was gone...."

"Garrett looked at them in silence for a time, and turning, went to the buckboard for a drink at the canteen. 'Well,' said he quietly, 'here's to the boys, anyway. If there is any other life, I hope they'll make better use of it than they did the one I put them out of.'" [29]

Garrett and Hough may have been surprised that Billy's grave no longer had a marker, but the grave had been unmarked for over 15 years, according to Colonel Jack Potter, who observed the original marker being stolen:

"The marker, Potter writes, was carried away in the late 80's and not destroyed or shot to pieces as generally supposed and as reported in various publications. Potter has been attempting to learn the whereabouts of the marker but has been unsuccessful."

"Potter was working for the New England Livestock Co. near Ft. Sumner when the directors of the company came out from the east for a visit."

"When they prepared to leave, they decided to visit the old cemetery and see Billy the Kid's grave."

"Potter accompanied them and recalled that the marker was lopsided as the bottom part of it had rotted away."

"The inscription put on it was 'Billy the Kid' with the date 'July 14, 1881.'"

"On the upper left hand corner was a small inscription in feminine hand: 'Dormir Bien Querido' (sleep well, dear one). There were about eight bullet holes scattered over the marker...."

"When the party of directors was ready to leave the cemetery, one named Chauncey, whose home was in Boston, said he was going to take the cross and put it in a museum."

"Potter said the man took the cross and carried it to the old Concord coach in which the party was riding."

"In the past few years Potter had traced the marker on it journey with Chauncey from Fort Sumner to Las Vegas, N. M., where Chauncey entrained with the marker strapped to his luggage."

"Potter has corresponded with relatives of two directors of the live-stock company through William Lyon Phelps, writer and Yale professor, but has been unsuccessful in obtaining further information regarding disposition of the marker. The two directors were with Chauncey on the trip to Fort Sumner." [30]

This was the first time Billy's grave marker was stolen – but it would not be the last.

48 ~ Chapter 2

Soldiers Moved from the Cemetery

On December, 2, 1905, just a few weeks after Garrett and Hough had visited Billy's grave, the administrator of military cemeteries for New Mexico announced that the cemetery at Fort Sumner would be closed.[31] The decision was motivated by a desire to consolidate all state military burials, plus a concern that further Pecos River flooding would entirely wash away the old cemetery. The *Albuquerque Journal,* in announcing the decision, noted:

> *"....some one will have a rather gruesome task, as all the bodies resting at present in the old post cemetery at old Fort Sumner, in this territory, are to be disinterred, reboxed and shipped to the national cemetery at Santa Fe, where they will be reinterred."*

> *"Not only the bodies of officers, but those of privates and civilians as well, who are buried at Fort Sumner, will be disinterred and shipped to Santa Fe, thus doing away entirely with the old Fort Sumner post cemetery, which is one of the oldest in New Mexico."* [32]

The original plan was to move all bodes from the cemetery. This was amended to moving only the military burials, because the government did not have the authority to remove the civilians buried in the cemetery. And further, residents with relatives buried in the cemetery did not want them removed.[33]

Bids were solicited for the transfer of the military bodies.[34] The contract was won by Charles W. Dudrow of Santa Fe, the lowest bidder, who agreed to do the job for $15 per body.[35]

On arriving at the cemetery, Dudrow found that although some of the military burials had wooden head boards, none were readable. Dudrow reported:

> *"...it was impossible to identify the remains of any particular person. I spent five or six days traveling through the country in search of old residents who might be able to identify some one or more of these soldiers, but after the lapse of forty years, it could hardly be considered possible to get reliable information as most of the old timers are dead and in a thinly settled country, such as this is, not much attention is paid to such matters."*

> *"I had an interview with a Dr. John Gayhart [Gerhardt] whom I traveled fifty miles to see who was a caterer for the officers' mess during the time of the post, but he could remember nothing regarding names of anything of that nature. He was, however, able to tell me the part of the cemetery used by the military. He also told me about the wooden monument over the remains of one of the Captains, but could not recall the name. I also found other parties who gave me practically the same information. At one time, so I was informed, all the graves of the soldiers were marked with wooden head boards and when I did this work some of them were still standing in the first and second rows, but all lettering entirely obliterated and not even legible under a magnifying glass."* [36]

Along with his account of painstakingly removing the bodies, Dudrow provided the military cemetery administrator with a hand-drawn map (see illustration). In addition to marking the locations of the soldiers' bodies, the map marks the location of Billy's grave, and the graves of his two *"gang"* members. This map provides the best historical documentation of the location of Billy, Bowdre, and O'Folliard's graves that exists. For a discussion of how this map affects the question as to whether Billy's grave is in the right location, see *"Is Billy's Grave in the Right Location?"* later in this chapter. To read Dudrow's complete account of locating and disinterring the bodies, see Appendix A.

The *Albuquerque Citizen* noted Dudrow's success:

> *"The bodies were disinterred, put into coffins and sent by teams to Santa Rosa. From there they were shipped over the El Paso and Southwestern to Santa Fe and will arrive Saturday, next, it is expected. There were twenty-two of them, and they will be placed in the National cemetery west of the city of Santa Fe."*

> *"The names, companies and regiments to which the soldiers belonged have been preserved, and will be placed on the headstones of their graves. Records of these are kept in the quartermaster's department in Washington and by super-intendent of the National cemetery in Santa Fe."* [37]

On the condition of the disinterred, Dudrow noted:

> *"The remains of each and every one were in a fine state of preservation and the entire skeleton of every one secured. The bones were dry and clean and no odor noticed except in one instance and then only very slightly."* [38]

That the much earlier military burials were not washed away by the 1904 flood is strong evidence that neither were the graves of Billy, Bowdre, or O'Folliard.

Fred E. Sutton Visits the Cemetery

In 1924 or 1925, Western writer Fred E. Sutton travelled to Fort Sumner seeking information on Billy the Kid. Wanting to visit Billy's grave, he sought out Deluvina Maxwell, who lived in a one-room adobe not far from the old fort:

> *"...old Deluvina volunteered to show the writer the grave of 'her boy.' We walked to the rude gate or entrance to the yard, from where there was a path running among the graves, and she said: 'Billy was buried three feet west of this path and thirty-one steps from the gate.' We stepped the distance and she pointed to a sun-baked, cracked and desolate spot of ground about six feet by three, as bare as it could be made, with grass and weeks growing to its very edge and then utterly refusing to go further. 'It has been this way always,' she said, 'and I don't see why things won't grow over Billy, for he was a good boy.'"* [39]

Deluvina died November 27, 1927. She received numerous obituaries, all of which noted her devoted friendship with Billy:

> *"Funeral services for Miss Deluvina Maxwell, aged servant in the family of L. B. Maxwell, New Mexico pioneer, will be held at the San Felipe Church in Old Town at 8 A. M. Tuesday. Miss Maxwell died here Sunday morning at the age of 80 after an illness of about two months. Deluvina Maxwell, a Navajo Indian, was captured by the Utes in 1856 when she was about nine years old. L. B. Maxwell, then living in at Cimarron, bought her from the Utes and gave her freedom, but she remained with the Maxwell family until her death."* [40]

50 ~ Chapter 2

> *"Miss Maxwell was brought to Albuquerque about two months ago when her health began to fail rapidly."* [41]

> *"...she mourned the death of the youth who she characterized as 'always good to those who treated him right.' Tales to the effect that Billy the Kid was not killed at that time were refuted by Deluvina Maxwell whenever she heard them."* [42]

Deluvina lies in an unmarked grave in the Santa Barbara section of the Mount Calvary Cemetery of Albuquerque. The records that would have permitted locating her grave are lost. [43]

"The Saga of Billy the Kid"

In January, 1926, Walter Noble Burns published *"The Saga of Billy the Kid."* The book was a huge success – perhaps the best selling non-fiction Western book ever written – and it revived intense, nation-wide interest in Billy's life. *"Saga"* was more accurate than Hough and Sutton's writings on Billy, because it was based on better research and lengthy interviews with numerous people who knew Billy, including Paulita Maxwell, Yginio Salazar, and John Poe. [44]

In *"Saga"*, Billy is portrayed as a robin-hood hero and Pat Garrett as a cold-hearted man-hunter. These characterizations, which went beyond the facts that Burns had gathered, were constructed from the myths and folklore that were already a large part of Billy's story in the minds of his interviewees. Burns added another appealing element to the story, one that has stuck to this day, that Billy was a committed defender of Hispanics in his actions. The resulting portrayal, combined with Burns' fine writing, created a tantalizing image of Billy the Kid that seized the public imagination. [45]

A new group of people began to visit Fort Sumner – Burns' readers – desirous of seeing Billy's grave.

Fort Sumner in 1926

Six months following the publication of Burns' book, a newspaper noted:

> *"Many tourists visit the cemetery annually but cannot find the grave without a guide."* [46]

Neither did the curious find much left of the old fort:

> *"Today, [the Fort's walls] are mere ridges in the grass. The outlines of the buildings can be traced. The parade ground is plainly visible, even to the butt of the flagpole still remaining. Pete Maxwell's house can be located, and even the room in which the Kid was killed. The cistern that was a distinguishing feature of Maxwell's house, furnishes a starting point for tracing out the house and rooms."*

> *"The Pecos, eating away at its bank, is fast obliterating old Fort Sumner. It has taken the ruins of the store building that were across from the post. It has taken the old saloon where Charley Foor, who also was postmaster, held forth."*

"It has eaten up the avenue and its rows of stately trees in front of officers' row. It has chewed away the gardens that were the pride of the place. It has gnawed right up to the concrete lip of the cistern that was Pete Maxwell's. Two and a half acres disappeared in the last rampage of the river. The next may take the cistern, the ruins of Maxwell's house, and the spot where the Kid met his death. It looks as if the Pecos is bent on wiping out this tragic place." [47]

Marking Billy's Grave

The surge of tourists led to a public call to mark Billy's grave. Burns added his voice to this plea in a widely-published 1926 interview:

"Despite his crimes, the memory of the boy outlaw is today cherished in affectionate regard throughout the southwest and New Mexico, it might seem, owes it to itself to place some sort of marker above his grave that has become a sort of shrine of romance. Otherwise, in a few years all knowledge of the exact location will be lost." – *Walter Noble Burns* [48]

The response was quick. By August, 1927, someone had put up a marker – but in the wrong place:

"In the old graveyard, now overgrown with range grass, there is a marker bearing the name of Billy the Kid. The story here is that the marker was misplaced and that – grim irony of fate – it adorns the grave of Joe Grant, one of the Kid's victims via the sixshooter. The Kid's own grave is nearby. Over in a far corner, in its own fenced enclosure, is the grave of Pete Maxwell."

"His body may be dead but his spirit seems to be hanging around these parts yet. He is a live topic in Fort Sumner. Tourists come from long distances to see the ruins of the old fort and to visit the graveyard." [49]

Here is another account of the marker, Billy's second, after the crude cross of fence slats:

"A fairly dignified octagonal marker, suitably inscribed with Billy the Kid's name and a few of the facts and dates concerning him, now appears at the head of one of the graves. At another is a broken bit of shovel blade. Nothing is at the third."

"But there is uncertainty. Some of the ancients of this locality claim the dignified marker is not at Billy's grave but at that of either Bowdre or O'Folliard; that Billy was buried in the middle, with his henchmen's bodies on each side of him, and that the rusty piece of shovel marks Billy's resting place. Others say not. They think the marker is where it belongs."

"So to get around dispute and at the same time give all three graves suitable recognition, it is proposed to erect a monument to all three knights of the six shooter." [50]

52 ~ Chapter 2

Locating Billy's Grave

In early April, 1930, four men – including three who had known Billy well – gathered in the Fort Sumner cemetery to locate Billy's grave:

> *"An interesting step was taken by the De Baca County Chamber of Commerce this week, when that body gathered together here A. P. (Paco) Anaya, of Vaughn, Jesus Silva, Vincente Ortega [Otero] and C. W. (Charley) Foor to make definite, the much-disputed location of the grave of New Mexico's most romantic outlaw, Billy the Kid, in the little cemetery at Old Fort Sumner."*

> *"These men located the grave in the old cemetery, and a picture of them was taken, standing at the foot of the graves of The Kid, Charley Bowdre, and Tom O'Fhalion. The Chamber of Commerce is having markers erected on the highway, directing tourists through the Valley roads to the cemetery, where a concrete curbing is in place around the three graves and a big concrete slab is to be placed over the grave of the Kid."* [51]

A. P. "Paco" Anaya was in Fort Sumner the night Billy was killed, and attended the funeral the next day.[52] Billy often stayed at the Anaya ranch, located at Cibello Arroyo a few miles south of Fort Sumner.[53] Paco's memoirs would later be published as *"I Buried Billy,"* a first-hand account of Billy's killing, death, and burial.

Jesus Silva was at Fort Sumner when Billy was killed. He attended the funeral and burial.[54]

Vincente Otero, a Pete Maxwell employee at the time, was in Fort Sumner when Billy was killed. He saw the body, attended the funeral, and dug the grave in which Billy was buried.[55]

Charles W. Foor was not present at Billy's burial, but he moved to Fort Sumner and made it his home a few months later.[56]

It would have been impossible to find four better choices then those named for the task of locating Billy's grave in April, 1930, given that such excellent witnesses of his burial as Pete Maxwell, Paulita Maxwell, and Deluvina Maxwell were dead. (Paulita died December 17, 1929 and was buried in the Fort Sumner cemetery.)

By mid-May, 1930, the three graves of Billy, Bowdre, and O'Folliard were surrounded by a concrete curbing, and a concrete slab was poured over Billy's grave. The cemetery grounds were enclosed in a wire fence.[57] The concrete construction was the work of J. T. Perkins.[58]

Did Anaya, Silva, Otero, and Foor identify the correct location? See the discussion later in this chapter.

A month later, a writer to the New Mexico highway department lamented that Billy's grave was too far from the highway to visit conveniently, *"...so I missed Billy's resting place."* [59]

King Vidor's BILLY THE KID

On October 12, 1930, Metro-Goldwyn-Mayer released BILLY THE KID. The movie was directed and produced by King Vidor. John Mack Brown played Billy and Wallace Beery played Pat Garrett. The movie was based on Burns' *"The Saga of Billy the Kid,"* and was the first movie to be made about Billy. The movie was a "talkie," a revolutionary technology that was only a year old in 1930.[60]

The movie was filmed partly in New Mexico, with several scenes shot in Lincoln, where Billy had escaped from the courthouse jail.[61]

The world premiere of BILLY THE KID was in Las Cruces, New Mexico, at the Rio Grande Theater. The 3-day showing was a tremendous success, with over 4,000 people attending:

> *"Those who looked at it were entranced.... But many left the house in tears, for we knew it is a historical fact that this so charming Billy had but a few days of life left to him. The Drama does not account of that, but ends with the youth riding rapidly in the direction of Mexico, followed by a very darling girl."*

> *"The monstrous crowds, and indescribable enthusiasm of those who saw the picture, certainly stamp it a winner. It is a world picture. Before many months it will be seen in London, Paris, Cairo, and other foreign cities."* [62]

The movie has a quintessential Hollywood ending – Billy is not killed by Garrett; rather, in the final scene, he rides off on his trusty horse into the black New Mexico night, leaving his fate to the imagination of the viewer.

The movie was hugely successful nationally. The combination of Burns' *"Saga"* and Vidor's BILLY THE KID secured for all-time the dual images of Billy the Kid as the Wild West's most famous gunman, and Pat Garrett as the Wild West's most-famous lawman.

Billy's Grave Marked

In late February, 1931, a granite marker was placed over the graves of Billy, Bowdre, and O'Folliard, at the location identified by Anaya, Silva, Otero, and Foor.[63] The marker had been ordered in late October, 1930.[64] This is the headstone that still marks the graves today. It is centered above the three graves. The top line reads:

PALS

Underneath that, in a left column are:

TOM
O'FOLLIARD
DIED DEC 1880

54 ~ Chapter 2

In a right column, separated by a vertical line are:

WILLIAM H.
BONNEY
ALIAS
BILLY THE KID
DIED JULY 1881

Centered under the two columns are:

CHARLES BOWDRE
DIED DEC 1880

The effort to pay for the gravestone was organized by Charles Foor:

"Funds to erect the monument were hard to obtain on account of objections that such action would make a hero out of the gunman. Billy the Kid has a record of killing 21 white persons and no count has been made of the number of Indians he killed."

"To refute stories of the good people that no grass would grow on Billy the Kid's grave, old-timers were photographed on the grave in knee-high grass." [65]

The story that Billy had killed 21 "white" people was false, but was not refuted by historical research at the time. Billy never killed any Native Americans. This was Billy's third marker.

With a permanent marker over Billy and his pals' graves and recognition as a historical site by the state of New Mexico, the Fort Sumner cemetery was a bona fide tourist destination. In July, 1932, the graves were visited by Johnny Mack Brown, of BILLY THE KID fame, and action movie star Douglas Fairbanks:

"In the small village of Fort Sumner, where the town was long divided over whether the mis-deeds and murders of young William Bonney should be glorified to posterity by fitting monument, the Fairbanks party spent last night. The historians of Fort Sumner finally won and today the grave of 'Billy the Kid' is prominently identified for inspection of visitors to Fort Sumner." [66]

"The party was conducted about Fort Sumner and vicinity by Charles W. Foor, authority on the record of the outlaw...." [67]

The pristine granite marker was soon being badly vandalized by visitors:

"'Souvenir Hounds' have left their marks in many places on the monument erected by public subscription to 'Billy, The Kid,' and his two pals, Charlie Bowdre and Tom O'Fallion...."

"Chunks from flat-size, down to small pebbles, have been knocked off the sides and top of the granite marker...."

"This marker was erected after many hundreds of such visitors had inquired why no suitable head-stone had been placed over the graves. The price of the marker was only raised after many attempts had failed to complete the

subscription price, and only then because Charlie Foor and a few other old-timers would not give up the effort to secure it."

"...Members of old-time families, when they view the depredations of the tourists, are much in favor of closing the little cemetery so such vandals cannot harm the graves of their own departed ones." [68]

Fort Sumner in 1937

In 1937, writer Dee Blythe visited Fort Sumner and reported:

"I went to Fort Sumner recently and looked up Chas. Foor, 80-year-old DeBaca county pioneer, who arrived there three weeks after the Kid was killed, while the town was still all riled up over the way that Garrett did it...."

"First we went to the old military cemetery, six miles southeast of the present town of Fort Sumner, where Billy the Kid and his pals, Tom O'Folliard and Charlie Bowdre, lie buried under one headstone, erected only in recent years. This headstone is already badly defaced by souvenir hunters and bids fair to go the way of all the other things connected with Billy the Kid...."

"In the same little cemetery where the Kid and his pals lie are the graves of the Maxwells, most powerful family in the history of the region. Pete Maxwell's grave has around it a little iron fence, built on a wall of rocks taken from the fireplace of the very room where Billy the Kid was slain while Maxwell lay helpless in his bed."

"[Mr. Foor] built the fence himself."

"[At the site of the old military post] I could see weed-grown, vaguely defined humps of clayish dirt that had probably been adobe walls at one time, but no outlines of buildings were to be seen. Even Mr. Foor was at a loss until we located the stump of an old tree that once cast its shade on the fort's parade ground. From there, old surveyor that he is, Uncle Charlie stepped off the exact location of every building."

"'Over there was the house the Kid stopped at the night he got killed.'"

"Here Charlie Foor interrupted his tale long enough to draw with his cane the location of every door and window in the room. He indicated the spot where the desperado fell." [69]

Charles Foor died January 3, 1940. He is buried in the Fort Sumner cemetery.

Cemetery Sold For Taxes and Plowed

On February 17, 1938, land adjacent to the Fort Sumner cemetery was sold in a tax sale for failure to pay county property taxes.[70] The county authorities and the new owner, John W. Allen, a Fort Sumner businessman, apparently believed that the property sale included the Fort Sumner cemetery.[71] This could not have been the case, however, because the Federal Government had specifically excluded the cemetery when it sold its last remaining land holdings in the Fort Sumner area on March 28, 1931:

56 ~ Chapter 2

> *"With the sale went all of the land which was once a part of the old fort and the Bosque Redondo Indian reservation. But two acres of the historic spot are left and that includes the old cemetery."* [72]

Allen immediately claimed ownership of the cemetery and fenced it in, preventing all access:

> *"I was in Ft. Sumner last Saturday and while I was eating in a restaurant I heard two tourist parties, each of the four or five members yellin' their heads off because they went down the valley to see the grave of Billy the Kid and they had found they were blocked by a five wire fence someone has built. The fence blocked them from getting to the exact spot to which they had travelled hundreds of miles."*

> *"And sure enough the fence is there."* [73]

Allen also prepared to cultivate the cemetery:

> *"Through the little cemetery the nose of a plow has chiseled an ugly ditch across the sacred plot. The occasion for the ditch is not known. Maybe it was for drainage purposes. Or maybe it was the first step in a plan to put the plot into cultivation."*

> *"This ugly furrow traverses the burial ground dangerously close to the rows of half-century-old crypts, among them the grave occupied by the body of Don Peter Maxwell, in whose sleeping room on July 14, 1881, Billy the Kid was shot and killed by Sheriff Pat Garrett, of Lincoln County. Rows of other graves are close by."* [74]

Fort Sumner families who had relatives buried in the cemetery were furious – both at Allen's callous treatment of the historic cemetery and at his unlawful denial of access to their loved ones' graves.

City – and state – outrage produced a call for a public meeting:

> *"The aid of Gov. Clyde Tingley has been enlisted and a mass meeting called for August 23 at the De Baca courthouse to formulate plans to recover the tiny weed-grown cemetery from J. W. Allen, Fort Sumner business man, who purchased the plot at a tax sale last spring."*

> *"Last week the marker on the Billy the Kid Grave was plastered with yellow handbills decrying the private ownership and calling citizens to the August 23 meeting."* [75]

Allen responded to the increasing public outcry by adding a gate to the cemetery fence and announcing plans to develop the old cemetery by enlarging it and selling new burial plots.

> *"But a large number of the people of Fort Sumner refused to accept the explanation and are loudly demanding the graveyard be removed from private ownership."*

"Leaders of the movement said they feared the new owner would commercialize the graves of the famous characters although they admitted Allen had not indicated such action...."

"Mrs. Adelina J. Welbourn, widowed granddaughter of Lucian Maxwell, plastered the town with handbills calling for a meeting at the courthouse August 23 to 'do something about' recovering the graves from their new owner."

"A committee headed by Mrs. Louisa Beaubien Barrett, another granddaughter of the Maxwell grant owner, and probate judge of De Baca county, conferred with Governor Tingley on the subject during his visit here last week. Other members of the committee were Mrs. Welborn, Frank Lobato, friend of Billy the Kid, Celestino Sandoval and Alfredo Lucero. The governor advised the group to work through the courts and promised his 'moral support.'" [76]

On February 11, 1939, Manuel Abreu, F. W. Spitz, and Kenneth Miller took legal action, asking the Tenth District Court to restrain Allen from making any *"further plowing or all other things"* within the Fort Sumner cemetery.[77] The three men had relatives buried in the cemetery.

The court granted the restraining request temporarily. Allen responded by stating that he had *"friends, but no blood relatives, buried in the said cemetery,"* giving him legal standing to ask the court to lift the restraining order permanently. He also asked that he be permitted to complete the irrigation ditch across the cemetery to a depth of six inches, construct other irrigation ditches as may be required, clear the cemetery land of mesquite trees, level it, and plant and irrigate grass. He further requested that he not be prohibited from selling new burial plots within the cemetery.[78]

Seventeen days later, the court issued a ruling:

"District Judge Harry L. Patton issued a permanent injunction Friday, prohibiting John Allen from 'molesting' or in any way changing the old Fort Sumner cemetery wherein Billy the Kid lies buried." [79]

Judge Patton ruled that the cemetery was public land and that Allen *"had no right, title, or interest in or to said plot of ground other than the rights as a member of the general public."* [80]

He also ruled further that:

"...the defendant [Allen], through no right whatsoever, had removed certain portions of the original fence which enclosed said plot of ground, and began plowing over the graves of the ancestors of plaintiffs and the other graves similarly situated and in addition ran an irrigation ditch three-fourths of the way across the cemetery." [81]

A few years later, Allen opened the Fort Sumner Museum, located next to the cemetery. This museum closed in 2018.

58 ~ Chapter 2

Billy Gets His Own Marker

On March 23, 1940, a stone dedicated just to Billy was placed at the foot of his grave. The date was selected *"so it would be in place for Easter Sunday."* [82]

The stone was a gift of John N. Warner, who owned a quarry and monument business in Salida, Colorado. Warner had become fascinated with Billy's lifestory and wanted to commemorate it with a descriptive marker. He contacted Fort Sumner and got the mayor's permission to install the marker.[83] Warner's daughter, reminiscing 36 years later, said, that to deliver the stone, the whole family packed their bags and drove in the family car from Salida to Fort Sumner, with the two hundred pound tombstone riding along beside her in the back seat of the car.[84]

The new marker was made of dark blue Colorado marble and was 23 inches high, 16 inches wide, and 6 inches thick. The stone inscription reflected what Warner believed about Billy. The top line reads:

TRUTH AND HISTORY

which appears over a carving of crossed pistols. The row below reads:

21 [21 marks representing carved bullets] MEN

Below that are:

BILLY
THE KID

Then in two columns are:

BORN
NOV. 23
1860
KILLED
JULY 14
1881

The last lines read:

THE BOY
BANDIT KING
HE DIED AS
HE HAD LIVED
ERECTED IN 1940 BY
J. N. WARNER MEMORIAL SERVICE
SALIDA COLORADO

The stone was cemented in place to prevent it from being stolen. This was Billy's fourth marker.

To protect the stones from souvenir hunters, *"extra heavy hard woven wire fencing, about 8 feet high, with sharp spiked top"* was placed around the graves.[85]

"The old granite marker, which has served as a magnet for every hard-boiled grave robbing hunter for the past few years, is practically destroyed as

a grave marker. Vandals have used nearly every sort of tool to cut loose, pry loose, every part of the top, sides and base of the old marker, until today it is liable to fall over, if the vandals leave it alone for a short while."

"[The marker] has served mainly as a magnet for every vandal who coveted a piece of the stone as a souvenir. They have even carried away gravel, pieces of wood, or any other object connected with the Old Fort Sumner burial plot."

"Old-time residents here, not to mention those of the old families who have their loved ones lying in the little former military cemetery, have long resented the actions of the tourists, who have carried off about everything movable in the burial plot." [86]

Lucien Bonaparte Maxwell Given a Stone

On May 29, 1949, at 2:30 p.m., a six-feet-high, four-and-one-half-feet-wide, memorial monument was unveiled over Lucien Maxwell's grave in the Fort Sumner cemetery.[87] Engraved on the stone was a map of Lucien Maxwell's land grant and facts about his life. The grave was unmarked previously.[88] Mrs. Adelina J. Welbourn, granddaughter of Lucian Bonaparte Maxwell, unveiled the monument at the dedication ceremony.[89]

The effort to mark Lucien's grave was led by the Colorado Historical Society, with the aid of the Historical Society of New Mexico. Much of Lucien's massive 2,000,000-acre, land-grant holdings before he purchased Fort Sumner were in southern Colorado, which had motivated the Colorado Historical Society to initiate the effort to honor him.

To ensure a legal right to install the monument, the Fort Sumner Rotary Club purchased the grave from Lucien's living relatives. [90]

The law generally recognizes that descendents have certain legal rights to their ancestor's graves, whether they were paid for or not (although today many commercial cemeteries require these rights to be signed away to be buried in their graveyard).

The monument was donated by Roy Erickson of the Denver Monument Company and designed by Wayne D. Gordon.[91]

Billy's Marker Stolen

On August 29, 1950, the dark blue marble stone donated by Warner was discovered to have been stolen:

"State Tourist Director Joe Bursey said today it learned of the theft through the curator of the Billy the Kid Museum...."

"Exact date of the theft is not known, but Bursey said the thieves apparently climbed over the fence, pried the stone loose and hoisted it outside."

"He said several men would be needed to lift the heavy marker over the fence." [92]

60 ~ Chapter 2

Lawsuit War to Move Billy to Lincoln

In April, 1961, the county commissioners of Lincoln County, New Mexico, sent a letter to the county commissioners of De Baca County requesting that the body of Billy the Kid be moved from Fort Sumner to Lincoln, stating as their primary reason:

> *"...the body of the Southwest's foremost personality should not be subject to exploitation for monetary purposes, but rather that it be re-interred in its rightful resting place, Lincoln County."* [93]

The letter added as a further reason:

> *"...the Old Lincoln County Courthouse, at Lincoln, was where Wm. Bonney was sentenced to hang for the murder of Sheriff Brady."* [94]

It is hard to imagine someone from Lincoln making this howler – but there it is.

To have any hope of getting Billy moved, the Lincoln County Commissioners needed a legal lever. They got it a few days later when a letter arrived from a Miss Lois H. Telfer, of New York City. She wrote:

> *"As a blood relative of William H. Bonney, both being in direct descent from Thomas Bonney, who came to America in 1634, may I offer any assistance to your request to have Billy's remains re-interred in Lincoln County."* [95]

Telfer explained her kinship to Billy by claiming that her (deceased) great-grandfather Orris Bonney was the twin brother to (deceased) William Bonney, who she claimed was Billy the Kid's grandfather.[96]

The problem: Billy's real name was Henry McCarty, not William H. Bonney, which had been disclosed in newspapers when Billy was killed, and also in Garrett's book, *"The Authentic Life of Billy the Kid."* William H. Bonney was an alias, picked by Billy from an unknown source for unknown reasons.

For reasons that she never made clear, Telfer was unconditionally committed to getting Billy's body transferred to Lincoln. At her own expense, she immediately travelled from New York to Lincoln, arriving on May 31.[97] She quickly hired attorney C. C. Chase, Jr., of Alamogordo – again, at her own expense – to pursue the action legally.[98]

At the same time, Lincoln secured another prominent supporter of the move – Wilbur F. Coe, son of Frank Coe. Frank Coe had been one of Billy's closest companions during Billy's life. Wilbur related that his father Frank had made a previous effort to move Billy:

> *"About 1925 my father made a special trip to Fort Sumner to see about moving Billy the Kid's body to Lincoln, where he considered it belonged. Due to expense of the operation and poor transportation facilities he was unable to carry out his plans."* [99]

Wilbur Coe's support for the "re-interment cause" was not surprising – he was president of the Lincoln County Historical Society.[100]

The De Baca County Commissioners' response was curt and unambiguous:

"We are not about to surrender it (the body) to his 'friends and relatives' who have waited this long to come forward and identify themselves." – Robert J. Coulter, Commissioner Chairman [101]

Attorney Chase's first action was to file a petition for the disinterment of Billy and his two pals, Bowdre and O'Folliard, with the Tenth District Court in Fort Sumner.[102] However, even as he was filing the petition, Chase told the press that he would seek to disqualify the sitting judge, Judge J. V. Gallegos, from presiding over the case because of very evident De Baca County political pressure.[103] Chase also filed a restraining order against the De Baca commissioners and Mrs. J. W. Allen, baring them from interfering with the disinterment.

Mrs. Allen was included in the restraining order because she owned the land surrounding the cemetery and the adjacent Fort Sumner Museum (Mr. Allen had died May 7, 1945.) [104]

At a large public gathering in Lincoln on May 30, the children of a number of men who had known Billy during his life spoke in favor of the re-interment: Margaret Salazar Bernardo, adopted daughter of Billy's good friend Yginio Salazar; Paul A. Blazer, grandson of Joseph Hoy Blazer, owner of Blazer's Mill, where Buckshot Roberts had been killed; Mayme Coe Perry, daughter of Billy's gun-fighting companion George W. Coe; and Allen Rhodes, son of Eugene Manlove Rhodes, famous western writer.[105]

Telfer offered more details about Billy's supposed father, William Bonney, stating that he had married Billy's mother in New York and had died in Kansas when Billy was just seven.

"She declared she was in no way interested in capitalizing on her relationship, wasn't writing a book or selling a movie, and that she was a cosmetologist. She wouldn't give the name of the company she represented as 'they might not like it.'" [106]

Residents of Fort Sumner with family members buried in the cemetery responded to Lincoln's call for Billy's removal with outrage. They laughed at Lincoln's claim that it would not commercialize Billy's grave, if moved, saying they expected the grave to be surrounded with *"glaring neon lights"* if Lincoln got it.[107]

On July 15, a relative of Charlie Bowdre entered the fray, requesting that Charlie's body not be disturbed:

"Today I read in a local newspaper that a Mrs. Lois Telfer is attempting to have the body of Billy the Kid disinterred and removed to a new site."

"I am hereby protesting such action. My cousin, Charlie Bowdre, is buried beside Billy."

"Although I'm not particularly proud of Charlie's nefarious activities, he was a member of our family and I would prefer to let well enough alone. According to reports I've learned that the graves can't be readily identified as to proper identification, therefore I'm concerned." – Louis A. Bowdre, Bartlesville, Oklahoma. [108]

62 ~ Chapter 2

On July 19, the De Baca commissioners filed a motion to dismiss the petition to remove Billy's body from the Fort Sumner cemetery.[109]

Ten days later, attorney Chase won his first victory. Judge Gallegos was replaced to hear the case by Ninth District Court Judge E. T. Hensley, Jr., by formal order of Chief Justice J. C. Compton of the New Mexico Supreme Court.[110]

On November 16, Judge Hensley held a hearing on the motion to dismiss the petition. Three witnesses were called by the defense, which argued that it was impossible to find the real location of Billy's grave, the present marker being only a "best guess," thus making re-interment impossible to achieve: [111]

> *"Carlos F. Clancy of Albuquerque testified he visited the graveyard prior to 1904, and there were no markings on the Kid's grave then."*

> *"Luciano Frank Silva, of Fort Sumner, said his grandfather, Jesus Silva, and two others marked the site for the present grave, although none could agree on the exact location of the original grave. They finally decided to put the marker in its present location...."*

> *"Walter F. Julian, a Fort Sumner mortician, told the court the last burial at the graveyard in 1946 required 'three or four tries' before an empty spot could be found."* [112]

No witnesses were called by Attorney Chase.

At the end of the hearing, Judge Hensley dismissed the motion to dismiss the petition, giving Telfer attorney Chase a second victory. [113]

On January 25, 1962, Judge Hensley granted a petition by Louis Bowdre to intervene as an affected party in the re-interment petition. In making this ruling, he stated:

> *"The court is not inclined to view with favor other petitions to intervene."* [114]

Only one witness appeared, J. T. Perkins. Perkins testified:

> *"...in 1930, a half-century after the Kid was gunned down by Sheriff Pat Garrett, he [Perkins] laid the curbstones around what passes for the Kid's grave. He said two old-timers instructed him."*

> *"Perkins said the two, who said they saw the burial, started at different landmarks and paced their ways to the spots they thought covered the short-lived outlaw. When they stopped walking they were still 12 feet apart...."*

> *"He said the old men finally compromised on the location and then argued about the position."* 115

On March 12, 1962, the long-delayed hearing on the re-interment petition finally began in the district court in Fort Sumner. At opening, both sides agreed to the stipulation *"that Mrs. Telfer is related to Bonney."* [116]

The defense explained that although they were well aware that biographers reported that Billy's real name was Henry McCarty:

"...they stipulated Miss Telfer's claim in order to avoid any possible future attempts to move the grave by others claiming relationship to Bonney." [117]

The only witness testifying was Louis Bowdre, who repeated his objection based on the impossibility of identifying the grave locations with any high degree of certainty. He explained his kinship with Charlie Bowdre by stating that Charlie was the son of Frank Bowdre, a brother of Louis' grandfather George W. Bowdre, Sr. Both sides accepted the stipulation that Louis was a relative of Charlie Bowdre. [118]

Miss Telfer had been expected to testify, but she did not show.

On March 13, Judge Hensley issued his ruling to a full courtroom: Billy would not be moved.

Judge Hensley gave two reasons:

"...due to the lapse of time and natural causes, it is no longer possible to locate the grave of said William H. Bonney."

"[Attempting to remove the body] would lead to disturbing the graves of others buried near him." [119]

The judge added:

"In the last days of his life, it became apparent that Lincoln County was the place he least desired to live and die." [120]

Attorney Chase told the press he would not appeal the decision. [121]

The trial publicity was a huge boon to Fort Sumner, greatly increasing tourist visits. Mrs Allen of the Fort Sumner Museum reported:

"I had my best February ever last month." [122]

Fort Sumner Park Created

On June 30, 1973, numerous state and city officials gathered at the old Fort Sumner site to dedicate the Fort Sumner Park and Museum. The effort to create a state park began in March, 1967, when a bond issue permitted the purchase of 130 acres from Mrs. John W. Allen. The land bought surrounded the cemetery and encompassed the grounds of the Fort. [123] The creation of Fort Sumner Park ensured that the historic site would be protected and freely open to the public.

A new, privately-managed Fort Sumner Museum was built next to the cemetery. The museum operated previously by Mrs. Allen had closed several years earlier.

Billy's Marker Returned

Twenty-six years after it was stolen, Billy's dark blue marble stone was returned to his grave.

In mid-July, 1975, Mr. and Mrs. Branham of Granbury, Texas, visited Billy's grave in the Fort Sumner cemetery and learned that the marker donated by Warner in 1940 had been stolen ten years after its installation, in 1950. They then spoke with Sophie Essinger, who was working at the nearby Fort Sumner Museum, telling her they were confident they knew where the missing stone was. [124]

64 ~ Chapter 2

In 1963, the Branhams had purchased a place outside of Granbury. In January, 1969, they sold the place to Gaylan Wright. Shortly after the purchase, Wright, while moving an old train boxcar on the place, uncovered what appeared to be the burial stone of Billy the Kid. He called the Branhams, who came out and looked at it. The Branhams had not known it was there when they sold their place. They said that as far as they were concerned, it was Wright's.[125]

On learning about the stone, Essinger visited Wright's place at Granbury, confirming it was the stolen marker. Through the cooperation of Wright and the sheriffs of the two involved counties, Hood in Texas and De Baca in New Mexico, permission was granted to return the stone to the Fort Sumner cemetery.[126]

Joe Bowlin, who owned the Fort Sumner Museum, drove to Granbury and returned with the stone on May 15, 1976.[127]

On June 19, 1976, at a public resetting ceremony as part of Fort Sumner's annual Old Fort Days, the stone was reinstalled at the foot of Billy's grave. The special guest of honor was Jarvis Garrett, Pat Garrett's son. To prevent it from being stolen again, the stone was secured with *"a steel band welded to a steel plate embedded in concrete."* [128]

When asked about the stolen stone, the Granbury sheriff said:

"How it got in that field is the ten thousand dollar question. It could have been there for the whole 26 years it was missing." [129]

Billy's Marker Stolen Again

On February 1, 1981, the marble stone donated by Warner was discovered to have been stolen again:

"The tombstone was last seen at 3:00 pm.... At 4:00 pm it was noticed missing."

"The De Baca County Sheriff's department reported no evidence at the scene. There were no tire tracks, footprints, and not a mark in the high chain link fence surrounding the burial site. The wind was blowing at high speeds throughout the day." [130]

The Fort Sumner Police issued a nation-wide bulletin to all law enforcement agencies providing details of the theft and a description of the missing stone. The theft was also reported in major newspapers across the country.

Ten days later, an anonymous caller contacted the Fort Sumner Police. He stated that he:

"...had attended a party at a house in Huntington Beach, near the ocean, that he'd seen the tombstone of Billy the Kid there, and that the host was a truck driver who sometimes passed through Fort Sumner." [131]

The truck driver was identified as Walter Nicolson, 25 years old. The Huntington Beach Police obtained a search warrant for the house, and a search led to the quick recovery of the stone:

"Detectives found the 40-year-old, 200-pound monument in Nicolson's bedroom...." [132]

Billy's Grave - "The Bivouac of the Dead" ~ 65

Nicolson was charged with larceny and burglary. But, evidently, the case was settled out of court as the Tenth District Court has no records of the case.

Is Billy's Grave in the Right Location?

The current location of Billy's grave is based on the authority of Anaya, Silva, Otero, and Foor, who picked the site in April, 1930. There were no surface indications of the grave then, so the men used remembered distances from remembered landmarks. This method of picking the site, based on estimation alone, has led many writers to conclude that the current location is wrong, possibly quite wrong.

Anaya, Silva, Otero, and Foor did not know of the Dudrow map when they selected their location. The Dudrow map only became known to historians in the 1990s. Dudrow supplied the map to the cemetery administrator with his report on the successful removal of the military burials from the Fort Sumner cemetery.

The Dudrow map shows the location of Billy's grave and two of his *"gang"* members. The obvious discrepancy between Dudrow's map and the graves as marked today is that the three graves are not in a neat row. One gang member's grave is located beside Billy's grave, as today, but the other gang member's grave is located several feet west and south of Billy's grave.

Dudrow successfully located the known military burials and made strenuous efforts to ascribe an identity to each set of remains, although he ultimately was unable to do so. He obviously was a meticulous worker. This gives his identification of Billy's, Bowdre's, and O'Folliard's graves formidable credibility.

Although not identified by name on Dudrow's map, the grave beside Billy's is almost certainly O'Folliard's, and the more distant grave is Bowdre's.

Mr. Scott Smith, Monument Manager of the Fort Sumner State Monument, carefully compared the location of Billy's grave on the Dudrow map with the location marked today. His conclusions are:

"The result of the comparison of the position of the current grave marker and the placement of Billy the Kid's grave as indicated by Dudrow in 1906 is that the current placement is consistent with the location marked on Dudrow's map. The measurements do not agree exactly because the cemetery was enlarged when the current wall was built, probably so that it would include the burials that Dudrow mentions being located between the original adobe wall and a surrounding barbed-wire fence."

"The cemetery seems to have grown by five or six feet on all sides. If I use the scale provided by Dudrow, his map would place the head of Billy's grave roughly 62 feet east from the dashed line representing the fence (west side of the cemetery); and the foot of Billy's grave roughly 99 feet west of the fence line (east side of the cemetery); and the center of the grave 46 feet south of the fence line (representing the north side of the cemetery). The actual measurements from the existing wall were 62 feet, 95 1/2 feet, and 49 feet, respectively."

"In other words, the current placement (based on information provided by Billy's pallbearers in 1930) is independently corroborated by Dudrow's map.

66 ~ Chapter 2

*According to my measurements, the grave might be a few feet further north or east, but the current marker is essentially in the right place." * [133]

Was Billy Really Killed?

The idea that Billy was not actually killed by Pat Garrett, but instead, a secret conspiracy was launched, in which Garrett and everyone else at Fort Sumner participated, has many believers.

This story first surfaced shortly after the January, 1926, publication of Burns' *"The Saga of Billy the Kid."* The story was started by an anonymous letter mailed in June, 1926, to the New Mexico Historical Society. The writer, an El Paso resident, claimed to know that Billy was alive and well:

"I know it to be a definite fact that the 'Kid' was not killed as reported, and that fact I have been position to prove for the past 16 years. I lived in New Mexico some 35 years and had an opportunity to learn something of its history."

"In the year 1900 I was visiting with an old timer who was present at the funeral and who declared that it was his belief that the 'Kid' was buried on that occasion. That aroused a suspicion in my mind and I set about to learn the facts in the case. It took me 10 years, but in 1910 I finally obtained the truth from two well known New Mexico characters, both intimate friends of the 'Kid' and also life-long friends of mine. One of them assisted in all the details of the 'Kid's escape. He loved the 'Kid' like a son, for he had brought him from Texas to New Mexico and had befriended him through all his troubles.

"The 'Kid' was well and alive in 1916, for I met him in company with one of those friends. There was a man killed all right, but it was not the 'Kid,' and furthermore, 'Pat' Garrett knew it was not the 'Kid' he had killed. I have no desire to get into public print, hence my name is not to be used in a public way. I would not object to telling how the 'Kid's escape was planned and effected, but not over my name yet." [134]

The contention of this letter was widely printed in the national press. Almost immediately people surfaced arguing both sides of the issue.

A supporter named Manuel Taylor stated he also had met Billy, in Guadalajara, Mexico, in 1914. He said Billy was married there and had a family. [135]

Another supporter named Leland V. Gardiner told the press:

"I am not certain, but believe I have seen the 'Kid'.... I am told that he is on an isolated ranch within 500 miles of El Paso."

"When strangers come to the ranch, the 'Kid' disappears until the visitors are gone. He was so well known in his day that he can't take chances on being detected." [136]

Burns' response was swift and emphatic, telegraphing the *Albuquerque State Tribune*:

"There are at least three persons still living at Fort Sumner, who knew Billy the Kid, intimately, and who saw him after he fell dead with a bullet through his

heart from Sheriff Pat Garrett's six-shooter. These are Mrs. Paulita Jaramillo, Manuel Abreu, and Deluvina Maxwell, an old Navajo woman, who for years was a servant in the Maxwell family."

"Mrs. Jaramillo, sister of Pete Maxwell and daughter of Lucien B. Maxwell... was one of the first to enter the room in which he met death and to view his body.... There certainly never was any doubt about 'The Kid's death in the minds of any of these." [137]

The response by those still living who had known Billy was unequivocal – Billy had been killed by Garrett – there could be no disputing it.

A. P. Anaya, the most authoritative living witness, stated in a press interview that *"there could be no mistake"* that Billy was dead:

"[He] not only was present in Fort Sumner at the time of the killing, but was a member of the jury that held an inquest over the body, and also helped to bury the body of Billy the Kid." [138]

Anaya also named the following people, all still alive at Fort Sumner, who saw Billy's body and could vouch for the *"details"* of his death:

"...Francisco Madina [Medina], Juan Madina [Medina], Mrs. Manuel Abreu, Cruz Trujillo, Santion Trujillo, D. Surbacker, Francisco Lovato, Vicente [Vincente] Otero, and Lavina Maxwell." [139]

Investigating the Billy-is-still-alive allegation, the *Albuquerque State Tribune* had a reporter in Fort Sumner interview Mrs. Manuel Abreu (Odila Maxwell), Paulita Maxwell Jaramillo, Deluvina Maxwell, and Frank Lobato, who all affirmed that they had seen Billy dead and buried.[140]

Charlie Foor issued a statement to the press in which he said:

"There need be no further controversy concerning this matter as there are numerous people yet living in this community who knew Billy the Kid intimately in life and viewed him in death and witnessed his funeral. I have lived here forty-four years and know the facts of his life and death and shall be pleased to cooperate with any representative you may send here for the purpose of securing affidavits relating to this controverted fact." [141]

Former New Mexico Governor Miguel A. Otero, Sr., who was *"writing a book about Billy,"* noted that he:

"...was at Fort Sumner in 1883, two years after Billy passed out with his boots on... and talked to a number of persons who were at the wake, including young women who had danced with him many a time, and he said today not one of them entertained a suspicion that there was a pinch-hitter at the funeral of Billy."

"Billy is as dead as a .45 through the heart could make him...." [142]

In spite of witness testimonies, the tale that Billy was not killed continued over the years to find un-dissuadable believers. This even led to contenders coming forward claiming to be the secretly-saved, un-dead Billy the Kid.

68 ~ Chapter 2

One reason for the tale's persistence is the 1940 movie THE OUTLAW, produced and directed by Howard Hughes, which ends with Garrett and Billy secretly colluding to bury somebody else in Billy's grave, enabling Billy to ride out of Fort Sumner without any fear of further pursuit.[143] This ending so angered the surviving members of the Garrett family that they sued Hughes for $250,000, alleging the film besmirched Pat Garrett's good name and character.

> *"Those bringing the action include Oscar L. Garrett of Houston, Jarvis P. Garrett, now in South America, and two daughters, Pauline Garrett of Dona Anna County, New Mexico, and Elizabeth Garrett, blind musician and poet of Roswell, New Mexico."*

> *"The character known as Pat Garrett in the film, it is contended, in no way depicts the true Pat Garrett, who is described as one of the men who finally brought law and order to the Western frontier."* [144]

If there had been a conspiracy to substitute another person's body for Billy's, it would have required the complicity of somewhere around two hundred people. These people would not only have had to maintain the "story" at the time of Billy's death, but for the remainder of their lives.

Pat Garrett submitted an official document on Billy's death, gave press interviews, and received about $7,000 dollars in reward monies. If it was all a fake, it strains credibility to believe that someone "in the know" would not have denounced him, perhaps out of financial interest, because Garrett would have been legally liable for a felonious fraud.

And Garrett would have had to spend the rest of his life worrying about Billy resurfacing, destroying his reputation, and placing him in legal jeopardy.

After starting the Billy-was-not-killed conspiracy with his (cowardly) anonymous letter, and receiving unsolicited support such as that offered to the press by Manuel Taylor and Leland V. Gardiner, the letter-writer was never publicly heard from again. By withholding his identify, the writer made it impossible to verify his claim of knowing two *"intimate friends of the 'Kid'"* who could describe the premeditated sham killing and explain how Billy's escape was prearranged.

The most exhaustive summary to date of the contemporaneous evidence that Billy was killed by Garrett was presented by Arizona Historian Dr. Robert J. Stahl in a petition that he submitted to the New Mexico Tenth District Court in 2013, and in a revised form in 2015. The petition requests that the court issue a formal death certificate for Billy, hoping thereby to end further speculation that Billy was not killed by Garrett. This petition can be read on the publisher's web site at:

http://doc45.com/pleading/tenth-court-pleading-by-dr-robert-stahl-for-kid-death-certificate.pdf

Photos

Replica of the first marker on Billy the Kids' grave. The original marker was made from two pickets from the wood fence surrounding Pete Maxwell's residence. Shortly after being erected, the marker was riddled with bullet holes, fired by a party of drunken soldiers. Replica by Colonel Jack Potter.

70 ~ Chapter 2

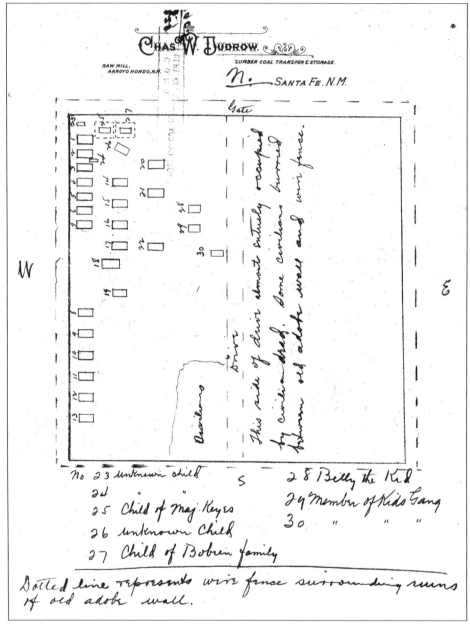

In January, 1906, Charles W. Dudrow contracted to move the military burials from the Fort Sumner Cemetery to the Santa Fe National Cemetery. He provided this hand-drawn map in his report to the cemetery administrator. In addition to marking the locations of the soldiers' bodies, the map marks the location of Billy's grave, and the graves of his two "gang" members. This map provides the best historical documentation of the location of Billy, Bowdre, and O'Folliard's graves that exists. Charles W. Dudrow, Letter to Col. C. A. H. McCauley, April 20, 1906, Fort Sumner Cemetery File, RG92, National Archives and Records Administration.

Second marker on Billy the Kids' grave, August, 1927. The octagonal marker *"was inscribed with Billy the Kid's name and a few of the facts and dates concerning him." Mountain States Monitor,* September, 1927.

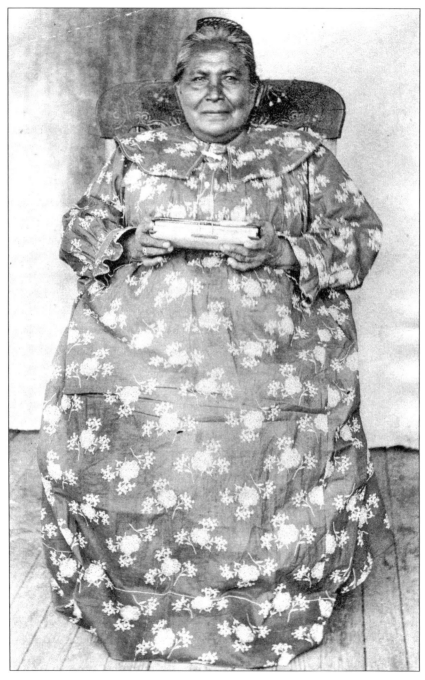

Deluvina Maxwell, shortly before her death on November 27, 1927. Courtesy Center for Southwest Research and Special Collections, UNM.

By mid-1928, Billy's grave is no longer marked. Courtesy Center for Southwest Research and Special Collections, UNM.

74 ~ Chapter 2

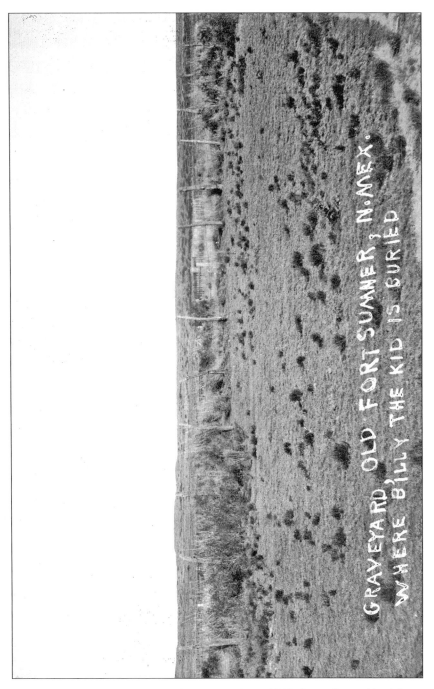

Looking toward the Fort Sumner Cemetery, about 1929. Arron Brown Harris' grave can be seen behind the fence. Courtesy Center for Southwest Research and Special Collections, UNM.

The grave of Arron Brown Harris (March 28, 1861 to November 13, 1925), about 1929. Courtesy Center for Southwest Research and Special Collections, UNM.

76 ~ Chapter 2

Pete Maxwell's grave, about 1929. The fence and wall surrounding Pete's grave were built by Charlie Foor. The rocks in the wall were taken from the fireplace in Pete's bedroom where Billy the Kid was shot. Courtesy Center for Southwest Research and Special Collections, UNM.

Billy's Grave - "The Bivouac of the Dead" ~ 77

Charlie Foor stands where Pete Maxwell's room was located, in the Maxwell house, at the spot – overgrown with grass and weeds – where Billy the Kid was killed. Undated photo. Courtesy Maurice G. Fulton Papers, Special Collections, UA.

Jesus Silva at Fort Sumner. Undated photo. Courtesy Maurice G. Fulton Papers, Special Collections, UA.

Charlie Foor stands at the location of Billy's grave at Fort Sumner. Undated photo. Courtesy Maurice G. Fulton Papers, Special Collections, UA.

80 ~ Chapter 2

Charlie Foor stands at Billy's grave while Captain Rey paces off the distance to the north gate of the cemetery. Undated photo. Courtesy Maurice G. Fulton Papers, Special Collections, UA.

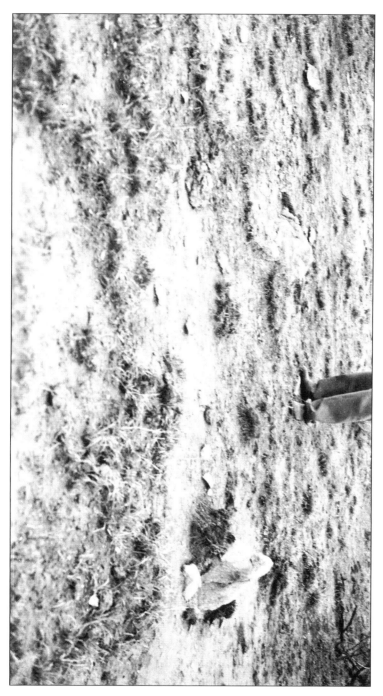

Billy's grave, marked in April, 1930, at the location identified by Charlie Foor, Paco Anaya, Jesus Silva, and Vincente Otero. Undated photo. Courtesy Maurice G. Fulton Papers, Special Collections, UA.

82 ~ Chapter 2

By mid-May, 1930, the three graves of Billy, Bowdre, and O'Folliard were surrounded by a concrete curbing, and a concrete slab was poured over Billy's grave. The concrete construction was the work of J. T. Perkins. Courtesy Maurice G. Fulton Papers, Special Collections, UA.

The world premiere of the Metro-Goldwyn-Mayer movie BILLY THE KID was held at the Rio Grande Theater, in Las Cruces, New Mexico, on October 12, 1930. Posed in front of the theater on opening day are the members of the State College marching band. Courtesy Archives and Special Collections, NMSU.

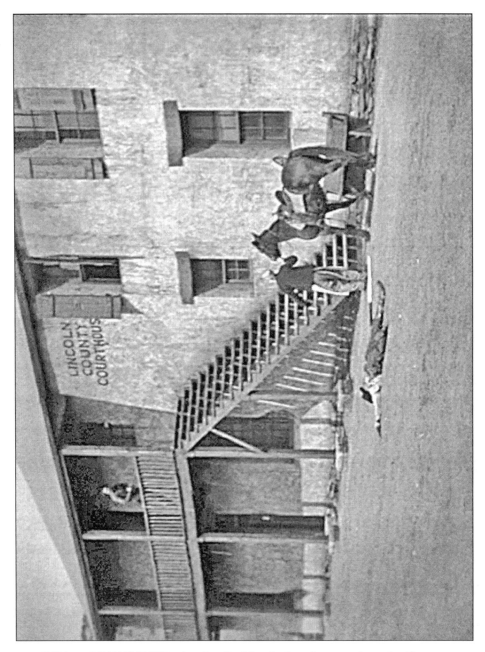

Still from BILLY THE KID, showing the Lincoln Courthouse, where the film was partially shot. Billy has just shot Deputy Marshal Robert Olinger, who is not only dead, but flattened.

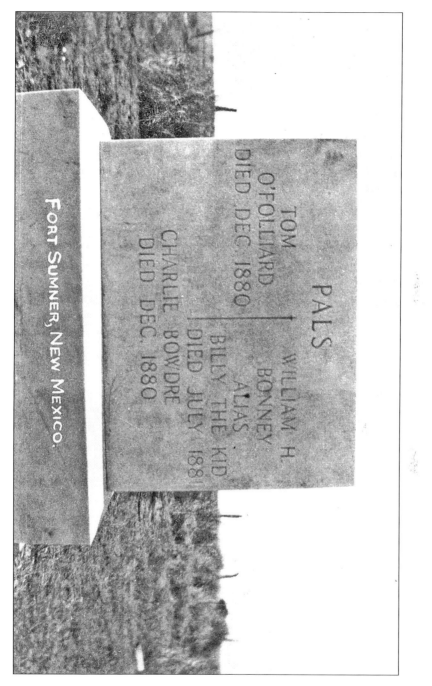

The stone marking the graves of Billy, Bowdre, and O'Folliard. The stone was installed in late February, 1931, at the location identified by Anaya, Silva, Otero, and Foor. Note that the stone has not yet been defaced by souvenir hunters.

86 ~ Chapter 2

Another photo showing the joint stone of Billy, Bowdre, and O'Folliard shortly after its installation. Courtesy Palace of the Governors Photo Archives (NMHM/DCA), 087479.

Billy's Grave - "The Bivouac of the Dead" ~ 87

A. P. "Paco" Anaya of Fort Sumner holding a photo of Billy the Kid on the 50th Anniversary of Billy's shooting by Sheriff Pat Garrett. July 14, 1931, Fort Sumner, New Mexico. Connaly, Courtesy Palace of the Governors Photo Archives (NMHM/DCA), 191559.

Side view of joint gravestone showing the handbill posted by Mrs. Adelina J. Welbourn, protesting the tax purchase of the Fort Sumner cemetery by John W. Allen. The Tenth District Court ruled that Allen had *"no right, title, or interest"* in the cemetery. *New Mexico Sentinel,* August 14, 1938.

Fort Sumner Cemetery as it appeared in August, 1938. *New Mexico Sentinel,* August 14, 1938.

90 ~ Chapter 2

The Fort Sumner Museum opened in 1940 by John W. Allen, located beside the Fort Sumner Cemetery.

The rival Billy the Kid Museum opened in October, 1952 in downtown Fort Sumner.

Photo shows the Billy the Kid marker donated by John N. Warner and installed on March 23, 1940. It has been stolen twice: once on August 29, 1950 and again on February 1, 1981. The first time the marker was missing for 26 years, the second time for 16 days.

Winter view of Billy's grave, January, 1947. Courtesy Fort Sumner Public Library.

94 ~ Chapter 2

Photo showing the vandalism of Billy the Kid's grave by an unknown person or persons in the early morning of June 16, 2012. Several other graves in the cemetery were also vandalized. Courtesy Tim Sweet, Billy the Kid Museum.

Chapter 3 | Cemetery Burials

You would not know it today, but the Fort Sumner cemetery is packed with burials – this chapter documents 112.[1] And it is highly likely there are many dozens of additional, undocumented burials. In 1961, Walter F. Julian, a Fort Sumner mortician, noted that:

> *"...the last burial at the graveyard in 1946 required 'three or four tries' before an empty spot could be found."* [2]

Julian was wrong about the last burial being in 1946 – the last burial was actually May 25, 2004, when Luciano "Chano" Frank Silva was buried in the cemetery. Frank was the son of Jesus Silva, who was present when Billy was killed. Chano's father and mother were buried in the cemetery, and he wanted to be buried there too. To achieve that, he found it necessary to obtain a court order. The same court order prohibited any future burials in the cemetery.[3]

Given the large number of burials, it is striking that there are so few grave markers. The cemetery contains just 25 markers, three of which commemorate children. There are also three markers commemorating multiple persons.

There are 16 burials closely connected to Billy the Kid.

Charlie Bowdre – friend and fellow warrior

Thomas O'Folliard – friend and fellow warrior

Luz Maxwell – knew Billy and was in Fort Sumner when Billy was killed

Pete Maxwell – friend in whose room Billy was killed

Emelia Maxwell – was in Fort Sumner when Billy was killed

Odila Maxwell – knew Billy and was in Fort Sumner when Billy was killed

Paulita Maxwell – likely girlfriend who was in Fort Sumner when Billy was killed

Manuel Abreu – friend who was in Fort Sumner when Billy was killed

Pablo Beaubien – friend who was in Fort Sumner when Billy was killed

Rebecca Beaubien – knew Billy and was in Fort Sumner when Billy was killed

Abrana Garcia – possible girlfriend who was in Fort Sumner when Billy was killed

Lorenzo Jaramillo – friend who was present when Billy killed Joe Grant. Was in Fort Sumner when Billy was killed, and served on the coroner's jury that ruled his death "justifiable homicide."

Jose Francisco Jaramillo – friend who was in Fort Sumner when Billy was killed. Later married Paulita Maxwell.

Isaac Sandoval – friend who was in Fort Sumner when Billy was killed.

Jesus Silva – friend who was in Fort Sumner when Billy was killed.

96 ~ Chapter 3

Also buried in the cemetery is Pat Garrett's first wife, **Juanita Martinez Garrett**.[4] Juanita married Garrett in November, 1879, at Anton Chico. Her father was Albino Martinez. Her sister was Celsa (Martinez) Gutierrez, one of Billy's possible girlfriends.

Juanita died within days of her marriage to Garrett, after becoming violently ill during the marriage celebration.[5] Two months later, Garrett married Apolinaria Gutierrez, daughter of Jose Dolores Gutierrez. Because Juanita's sister Celsa (Martinez) Gutierrez had the same last name as Apolinaria Gutierrez, many writers have assumed that Juanita and Apolinaria were sisters – that Garrett had married Juanita's sister after her death. Not true. Celsa Martinez became Celsa Gutierrez by marrying Sabal Gutierrez (probably in 1877). [6]

Military Burials

When Dudrow removed the military burials from the cemetery in 1906, he worked from official Fort Sumner records. Those records indicated that between 1863 and 1868, while Fort Sumner was an operational fort, the following men were buried in the cemetery (in death date order):

Samuel Strunk, Pvt., 1st N.M. Cavalry, killed by Indians January 2, 1863, #691.

Marcus Cruiz, Pvt., 1st N.M. Cavalry, died of intermittent fever, October 5, 1864, #677.

Albertin Crutchfield, Pvt., 1st CA. Cavalry, cause of death unknown, December 8, 1864, #678.

Robert Lusby, Capt., A. A. G. U.S. Volunteers, took by mistake a vial of poison, February 20, 1865, #689.

Juan Chavez, Pvt., 1st N.M. Cavalry, died of pneumonia, March 30, 1865, #694.

Philip Welsh, Hospital Stewart, 1st N.M. Cavalry, delirium tremens, April 25, 1865, #693.

Joseph Berney, Capt., 1st N.M. Cavalry, cause of death unknown, October 7, 1865, #674.

William Dougherty, Pvt., 1st CA. Cavalry, congestive fever, December 7, 1875, #680.

Juan Marcus, Pvt., 1st N.M. Cavalry, pneumonia, December 21, 1865, #690.

Patrick Toury, Pvt., 5th U.S. Infantry, apoplexy, July 7, 1866, #692

Patrick Johnson, Pvt., 5th U.S. Infantry, accidentally shot by comrade, January 15, 1867, #686.

Hugh Friel, Cpl., 3rd U.S. Cavalry, died from acute rheumatic fever, May 3, 1867, #683.

William C. Edwards, Cpl., 3rd U.S. Cavalry, shot by a comrade near Puerto de Luna, June 13, 1867, #681.

William J. Eckley, Lieut., 5th U.S. Infantry, central congestion, June 20, 1867, #695.

John Devine, Pvt., 3rd U.S. Cavalry, killed with arrows in a skirmish with the Navajos, July 9, 1867, #679. (Devine, Cook, White, Kerr, and Lee were killed on a hill overlooking Fort Sumner. Companies G and I, 3rd Cavalry, had been sent to recover horses believed to have been stolen by a band of Navajos led by Chief Narbono. The soldiers evidently fired first, starting the conflict in which five soldiers were killed.[7])

James Cook, Pvt., 3rd U.S. Cavalry, fight with Indians near Fort Sumner, July 9, 1867, #676.

Edward White, Pvt. 3rd U.S. Cavalry, fight with Indians near Fort Sumner, July 9, 1867, #682.

William Kerr, Pvt., 3rd U.S. Cavalry, fight with Indians near Fort Sumner, July 9, 1867, #687.

John Lee, Pvt., 3rd U.S. Cavalry, fight with Indians near Fort Sumner, July 9, 1867, #688.

Edward Johnson, Citizen, employee in Quartermaster Dept., killed while resisting arrest, October 12, 1867, #685.

Thomas Hedgecook, Pvt., 37th U.S. Infantry, cause of death unknown, November 17, 1867, #684.

William Epple, Pvt., 3rd U.S. Cavalry, cause of death unknown, February 1, 1868, #675. [8]

On March 8, 1906, these men were re-buried with military honors in the Santa Fe National Cemetery. With the exception of Lieutenant William J. Eckley, none of the remains could be identified. A name was arbitrarily assigned to the other sets of remains, and given a stone marker. The number of each man's marker follows the man's death date in the list above.[9]

Dudrow also noted the cemetery contained the burials of five children, three unidentified, one the child of a Bobien [Beaubien] family, and one the child of Major Alexander and Virginia (Maxwell) Keyes. Virginia was the oldest daughter of Lucian Maxwell.[10]

Maxwell Family

Lucien Bonaparte Maxwell, his wife, and five of their children are buried in the cemetery.

Lucien Bonaparte Maxwell (September 14, 1818 – July 25, 1875). Lucien has a large monument in the cemetery, placed over his previously unmarked grave on May 29, 1949. To ensure a legal right to install the monument, the Fort Sumner Rotary Club purchased the grave from Lucien's living relatives.[11] The monument was donated by Roy Erickson of the Denver Monument Company and designed by Wayne D. Gordon.

What is known today as the Maxwell Land Grant was granted by Mexico to Carlos (Charles originally) Beaubien and Guadalupe Miranda. Carlos Beaubien was an American who had entered New Mexico as a trader and trapper, and adopted Mexican citizenship. Guadalupe Miranda was the secretary to the Governor of the Mexican Territory of New Mexico. It is certain that the Mexican government would not have made the grant to Beaubien alone. Miranda fled to Mexico when the Mexican-American War began, and

98 ~ Chapter 3

following the victory of the Americans, sold his share of the grant to Beaubien. Lucien married Beaubien's daughter, María de la Luz Beaubien on March 27, 1842. Lucien obtained the grant he became famous for through the inheritance of his wife Luz and by purchasing the shares of the grant that Luz's brothers and sisters inherited.

Maxwell sold the Maxwell Grant in 1870. At that time he was probably the richest man in New Mexico. He purchased the grounds and buildings of Fort Sumner on October 17, 1870.

Lucien's obituary noted the respect in which he was held by his contemporaries:

"Lucien B. Maxwell died at his residence, at Fort Sumner, in the county, at 2 o'clock Monday morning, the 26th instant. His illness was sudden and a messenger was dispatched to this place, a distance of one hundred and fifty miles, for the medical assistance of Dr. J. H. Stout. Relays of horses were provided at various points on the road, and the Doctor started early on Monday morning for Fort Sumner, but on reaching Elkins' ranch, on the Pecos, eighty miles from town, he learned of the death of Mr. Maxwell and returned."

"Lucien B. Maxwell was one of the first American settlers of New Mexico, and his life has been intimately connected with the early history of Colorado and this Territory. He was a companion and associate of St. Vrain, Chas. Bent, Kit Carson, Richard Owen, and others of that band of pioneers who penetrated to this country prior to its acquisition by the United States, and who were remarkable for their natural ability and force of character. Against Lucien B. Maxwell no man can say ought and he died after an active and eventful life, probably without an enemy in the world. Of few words, unassuming and unpretentious, his deeds were the best exponents of the man. He was hospitable, generous and upright, and dispensed large wealth, acquired by industry and genius, with an open hand to the stranger and to the needy. No one in want, whatever his condition in life, whether Indian, Mexican, or American, ever crossed his threshold without being the recipient of his bounty...." [12]

It is surprising that a person as rich and prominent as Lucian Maxwell was not quickly commemorated with a grave stone. No grave marker for the dead was a family habit, however.

María de la Luz Beaubien Maxwell (June 28, 1829 – July 13, 1900), wife of Lucien Maxwell, is commemorated on a small Abreu family stone. The joint stone was placed in the cemetery in the 1960s. Luz married Lucien at the age of 13 on May 27, 1842.

Luz's obituary noted:

"Mrs. Luz B. Maxwell, widow of Lucien B. Maxwell, of the Maxwell land grant, died at Fort Sumner on the 13th inst., at the age of 71 years and 20 days of paralysis.... The funeral occurred on the following day. She was the daughter of Carlos Beaubien, a sister to the wife of the late Jesus Abreu, of Rayaldo, N. M., and went to Fort Sumner with her husband in 1870. She was the mother of six children...." [13]

Peter "Pete" Menard Maxwell (April 27, 1848 – June 21, 1898), oldest child of Lucien and Luz Maxwell.

Pete is the only Maxwell commemorated by a grave stone at the time of his death. Hard to read today, the stone is inscribed:

> In memory of
> PETER MAXWELL
> Born
> April 27, 1848
> Died
> June 21, 1898
> No pains no griefs no
> Anxious fears
> God reach our loved one
> Sleeping here

Enclosing Pete's grave is an iron fence built on a wall of rocks. The fence and wall were built by Charlie Foor. The rocks in the wall were taken from the fireplace in Pete's bedroom where Billy the Kid was shot. These rocks are the only things that remain of the Maxwell residence at Fort Sumner.[14]

Pete's obituary was surprisingly brief:

> *"By parties arriving from Fort Sumner it was learned today that Peter Maxwell died at his home, near that place, on the morning of the 21st, and was buried on the following day. He leaves a wife and one child. Peter Maxwell was the son of Lucien B. Maxwell, the original owner of the celebrated Maxwell land grant, lying in Colorado and New Mexico. Peter Maxwell is well remembered in this city, where he was a frequent visitor in years past."* [15]

Pete married Sarah "Sadie" C. Lutes on November 29, 1884, the same day Charlie Foor married Silberia Beaubien. Nothing is known of his reported child. Six months after Pete's death, Lutes married James F. Wade.[16]

Emelia Maxwell (1852 to 1884). Commemorated on the Abreu family stone. Emelia married Manuel Fernando Abreu in 1879. When she died, Manuel married her sister Odila.

Odila Bernice Maxwell (July 25, 1868 to May 5, 1935). Commemorated on the Abreu family stone. She became Manuel Fernando Abreu's second wife on August 16, 1887.

Odila's obituary noted:

> *"Mrs. Odila Bernice Abreu, wife of the late Manuel Abreu, died Sunday afternoon at the Pecos Valley Hotel in Fort Sumner; the family have resided at Old Fort Sumner for more than forty years."*

> *"Mrs. Abreu was born July 25, 1868 at Cimarron, New Mexico, and was united in marriage in 1886 with Manuel Abreu, and to this union were born five daughters and two sons, all of whom survive their parents... burial [was] in the Old Fort cemetery where the husband and father are buried."* [17]

100 ~ Chapter 3

Note: Although birth records indicate Odila Bernice Maxwell, she appears to have gone by Odila, and her grave marker and her obituary identify her that way.

Paulita (Paula) Maxwell (January, 1864 to December 17, 1929). Commemorated on the Abreu family stone. Paulita married José Francisco Jaramillo on January 14, 1882.

Paulita is the primary candidate for Billy the Kid's girlfriend, as discussed in the first chapter.

Paulita's obituary noted her connection to Billy:

> *"Mrs. Paula Maxwell Jaramillo, aged 65, died at her home here, Tuesday, and was buried Wednesday afternoon in the cemetery at Old Fort Sumner, beside the grave of her brother Pete Maxwell."*

> *"Mrs. Jaramillo had been in poor health for many years with Bright's disease, and her death was not unexpected by her family and friends...."*

> *"Mrs. Jaramillo was noted for her beauty and wit as a young lady, and was present in her brother's home on the night in July, 1881, when Billy the Kid was killed by Pat Garrett...."* [18]

Julian Maxwell (1857 to 1877). Commemorated on the Abreu family stone. Julian, a Cheyenne, was adopted while a young boy by Lucien and Luz Maxwell.

Bonney, Bowdre, and O'Folliard

William Henry McCarty, alias William H. Bonney, alias William Antrim, alias Billy the Kid (1859 to July 14, 1881). Commemorated on two stones: a joint marker with "Pals" Charlie Bowdre and Tom O'Folliard and a foot stone donated by John N. Warner.

In May, 1930, a concrete slab was poured over Billy's grave, and the three graves were surrounded with a concrete curb. Both were the work of J. T. Perkins. The joint marker was erected in February, 1931. The foot stone was erected on March 23, 1940. The cement slabs over Bowdre and O'Folliard's graves were placed there in 1973.[19]

Billy's birth date and birth place are in dispute. A likely date, accepted by many historians, is November 20, 1859, in New York City. The foot stone gives Billy's birth date as November 23, 1860, a date almost universally rejected today.

Thomas O'Folliard, Jr. (1858 to December 19, 1880). Commemorated on a joint stone with Billy the Kid and Charlie Bowdre.

O'Folliard was killed by Garrett and his posse seven months before Billy was killed. Billy and five compadres – Thomas O'Folliard, Charlie Bowdre, Billy Wilson, Dave Rudabaugh, and Thomas Pickett – rode into Fort Sumner in the evening of December 19, 1880. They were on the run from Garrett, who was seeking to arrest them for the murder of Sheriff Brady. O'Folliard intended to visit his wife, who lived in Fort Sumner, and Billy and the others expected to spend the night in a place they considered safe. But Garrett and his posse were waiting for them. While still on horseback, Billy's group was challenged to surrender. When they did not, a firefight resulted in which O'Folliard was killed. Although not certain, it is likely that it was Garrett who fatally shot O'Folliard.

A nearby resident, Manuel Brazil – who Billy considered a friend – had "snitched" on Billy, telling Garrett that Billy was visiting Fort Sumner regularly. This is the same

Manuel Brazil who sent Garrett the letter that led to Garrett's trip to Fort Sumner on July 14, 1881, which, of course, resulted in Garrett's finding and killing Billy.

Charles Meriwether Bowdre (1848 to December 23, 1880). Commemorated on a joint stone with Billy the Kid and Tom O'Folliard.

Charlie Bowdre was also killed by Garrett and his posse. Following the killing of O'Folliard at Fort Sumner, Billy, Bowdre, Wilson, Rudabaugh, and Pickett fled to a nearby ranch owned by Thomas Wilcox and Manuel Brazil. Then, not feeling safe at the ranch, they decided to take refuge at a place where Billy had hid out before – an isolated, abandoned rock house located about 20 miles from Fort Sumner. In the early morning of December 23, Garrett's posse silently surrounded the rock house.

Just at daylight, the men in the rock house were heard getting up. Suddenly, one man emerged, intending to feed his horse. Here accounts differ. One is that the man was shot without warning, being mistaken for Billy. The other is that he was ordered to surrender, but drew his pistol instead. Whichever the case, the man – who turned out to be Charlie Bowdre – was blasted by a volley of shots, leaving him fatally wounded.

Abreu Family

Many members of the Abreu family followed Lucian Maxwell to Fort Sumner in 1870.

Manuel Fernando Abreu (January 11, 1857 to July 12, 1925). Commemorated on the Abreu family stone. Manuel married Emelia Maxwell in 1879, and following her death, married Odila Maxwell in 1887.

Manuel Abreu was the sheep foreman for the Maxwell operation in Fort Sumner. He was a witness to Garrett's wedding to Apolinaria Gutierrez in Anton Chico. He was at Fort Sumner when Billy was killed, and attended Billy's funeral and burial.

Following Pete Maxwell's death, Manuel Abreu became a big sheep rancher himself, owning over 14,000 head in 1915.[20]

Manuel had an extensive obituary in the Fort Sumner Leader, but it has been clipped out of the sole surviving newspaper copy, making it unavailable.

Manuel Fernando Abreu, Jr. (September 18, 1895 to March 26, 1940). Commemorated on the Abreu family stone. Also commemorated with his own stone which has the wrong birth year (1898). Manuel F. Abreu, Jr., was the son of Manual F. Abreu.

Manuel's obituary noted his burial in the Fort Sumner cemetery:

"Funeral services for Manuel F. Abreu, 42, De Baca county pioneer, were conducted in Albuquerque Wednesday. The body was brought to Fort Sumner for interment in the family plot in the old Fort Sumner cemetery Thursday afternoon...." [21]

Alfredo Napoleon Abreu (May 12, 1894 to September 18, 1962). Commemorated on the Abreu family stone. Alfredo was the son of Manuel F. Abreu.

Luz Berenisa Abreu (August 16, 1890 to May 31, 1936). Commemorated on the Abreu family stone. Luz Berenisa was the daughter of Manuel F. Abreu. She never married.

102 ~ Chapter 3

Amalia Mares Abreu (August 7, 1876 to May 24, 1962). Commemorated on the Abreu family stone. Amalia married Manuel F. Abreu's brother Jesus L. Abreu in 1893.

Enriques Abreu (??). Commemorated on the Abreu family stone. No information found.

Beaubien Family

Many members of the Beaubien family followed Lucian Maxwell to Fort Sumner.

Pablo C. Beaubien (August 24, 1849 to 1903). Commemorated with a stone. Brother of Luz Beaubien Maxwell and Juan Christobal Beaubien. Married Rebecca Abreu Beaubien on August 6, 1870. Pablo was in Fort Sumner when Billy was killed and saw the body.

Rebecca Abreu Beaubien (August, 1855 to 1932). Commemorated with a stone. Wife of Pablo C. Beaubien. Rebecca was in Fort Sumner when Billy was killed and saw the body.

Juan Christobal Beaubien (August 24, 1848 to 1901). Brother of Pablo C. Beaubien and Luz Beaubien Maxwell. Father of Severo Beaubien, Filipe Beaubien, and Silberia Beaubien Foor. Married Maria Albina Beaubien.

Maria Albina Trujillo Beaubien (1850 to ??). Wife of Juan Christobal Beaubien. Mother of Severo Beaubien, Filipe Beaubien, and Silberia Beaubien Foor.

Severo Beaubien (1879 to Jan 10, 1931). Son of Juan Christobal Beaubien and brother of Beaubien Silberia Foor.

Felipe Beaubien (1884 to January 29, 1902). Son of Juan Christobal Beaubien and brother of Silberia Beaubien Foor. Felipe was murdered in a violent robbery.

About 6:45 in the evening of January 29, 1902, four men burst into the Pecos Mercantile Company, which also housed the Fort Sumner Post Office (Charlie Foor, the postmaster, was present).

Philip Holzman, manager of the Pecos Mercantile, gave this first-hand account:

> *"Rushing in with pistols and Winchesters, two in each hand, and covering us with the same, demanded 'Hands up,' and covered all the men who were in the store.... After that I had to surrender to them whatever they wanted. They took all the cash in the safe.... They then helped themselves to anything they wanted in clothing, blankets, furnishing goods, hats, canned goods and grain. They did as they pleased. They took all my cartridges...."*

> *"They stayed in the store an hour and a half. Meantime, people kept coming into the store and they made them surrender everything they had on their persons. They got seven pistols and three watches besides my watch and chain and about $400 or $500 from those people who came in and from the store...."* [22]

Felipe was killed in the initial seconds of the robbery:

> *"A 12-year-old boy, named Felipe Beaubien, an assistant in the post office, was seized with abject fright when the outlaws entered the store, fled precipitately, and was shot dead, the bullet coursing through his brain."* [23]

Four men were tried for the robbery and murder: George Cook, Whit Neal, George Massegee, and John Smith. Massegee, who confessed to his part in the crime, testified:

"It was agreed that the first man to make a break was to be shot at once... and then they would not have as many to kill...."

"It was only a minute or so after the robbers entered the store that he [Massegee] heard a shot, and it was this shot that evidently killed young Beaubien." [24]

Cook and Neal were sentenced to life in prison. Massegee and Smith were sentenced to five years in the penitentiary.[25] Both Massegee and Smith were released for good behavior after serving four years.[26]

Paul C. Beaubien (December, 1893 to 1929). Commemorated with a stone. Son of Juan Christobal Beaubien and brother of Silberia Beaubien Foor.

Concepcion Beaubien (??)

Foor Family

Charles Wesley Foor (December 12, 1850 to January 3, 1940). Commemorated with a stone, which incorrectly gives 1-20-40 as his death date. Married Silberia Beaubien Foor October 29, 1884. The stone reads: *"Early settler came to New Mexico in 1880."*

"Death claimed Charlie Foor, 89, the oldest resident of Fort Sumner and one of its most colorful pioneers, last night at the home of a daughter here."

"Foor, a recognized authority on the history of Billy the Kid, fell and broke a leg last summer. He never fully recovered from the injury."

"Foor was a vital part of the colorful history of Fort Sumner.... It was Foor who plotted the townsite of the present Fort Sumner. At one time he was postmaster at the old fort, and served as justice of the peace...."

"Burial will be in the Fort Sumner cemetery." [27]

Silberia Beaubien Foor (July, 1869 to 1915). Commemorated with a stone. Silberia was a Native American who was adopted while a young girl by Juan Christobal Beaubien and Maria Albina Beaubien. The stone reads: *"Wife of Charles W. Foor raised by Indians Mother of Eight."*

Garcia Family

Nipomocino Garcia (April 1835 to ??). Husband of Francisca Garcia.

Francisca Garcia (May 1850 to ??). Wife of Nipomocino Garcia.

Abrana Segura Garcia (December 1859 to 1932). There is a long tradition among the descendents of Abrana that she was Billy's girlfriend, and even that she had a son by him. They report that she was Native-American and possibly related to Deluvina Maxwell.

She was adopted and raised by Fernando and Manuel Segura as Abrana Segura.

In 1881 when Billy is killed, she is married to Martin Garcia. They have three children living with them: Antonio, aged 7 years; Ricardo, aged 5 years; and Navora, aged

104 ~ Chapter 3

five months. Antonio and Ricardo are Martin's children from a previous relationship. Navora is Martin and Abrana's child.

Navora Garcia (1880 to November 14, 1941). Daughter of Martin and Abrana Garcia.

Reveca [Rebecca] Garcia (1881 to ??). Daughter of Martin and Abrana Garcia.

Rose Garcia (1883 to ??). Daughter of Martin and Abrana Garcia.

Isidora Garcia (??)

Gonzales Family

Many members of the Gonzales family followed Lucian Maxwell to Fort Sumner.

Rumaldo Gonzales (March, 1875 to January 17, 1925). Commemorated with a stone.

Juanita S. Gonzales (March, 1884, April 11, 1940). Commemorated with a stone. Wife of Rumaldo Gonzales.

Jose J. Gonzales (1883 to ??). Son of Rumaldo Gonzales.

Montoya Gonzales (??).

Juan N. Gonzales (1866 to ??).

Harris Family

Arron Brown Harris (March 28, 1861 to November 13, 1925). Commemorated with a stone. The wood fence initially around his grave is long gone.

Harris moved to Fort Sumner in 1882. He worked in the cattle business until 1895, when he opened a mercantile business.[28]

Emma Harris (September 19, 1895 to April 4, 1918). Commemorated with a stone. Daughter of Arron Brown Harris.

> *"Miss Emma Harris, daughter of Mr. and Mrs. A. B. Harris, died at her home in this place Thursday morning. She suffered an attack of pneumonia on Monday, dying three days later. Deceased was about 23 years of age and had lived in this vicinity all her life, having been born at the 'Old Fort.'"* [29]

Arron Brown Harris, Jr. (March 5, 1908 to May 7, 1912). Commemorated with a stone. Son of Arron Brown Harris.

> *"The little 4-year-old boy of Brown Harris, of Fort Sumner, was drowned in an irrigation canal near the family home last Tuesday evening. The boy, in company with other boys, was playing along the canal and the unfortunate lad is supposed to have fallen in. The water is very swift at this point and the lad being too weak to battle against the current was soon drowned. His comrades, through excitement, were unable to tell how the distressing accident happened."* [30]

Edward B. Harris (1916 to 1922). Commemorated with a stone. Son of Arron Brown Harris.

Jaramillo Family

The Jaramillo family was the second richest family in the Fort Sumner area.

Lorenzo Jaramillo (September, 1845 to May 3, 1914). Was present when Billy killed Joe Grant. Served on the Billy the Kid's coroner's jury. Brother of Jose Francisco Jaramillo, who married Paulita Maxwell.

Jose Francisco Jaramillo (June 12, 1862 to March 27, 1937). Was in Fort Sumner when Billy was killed. Brother of Lorenzo Jaramillo. Married Paulita Maxwell on January 14, 1882.

Clemente Jaramillo (May, 1830 to ??).

Lola (Dolores) Jaramillo (1871 to ??). Daughter of Lorenzo Jaramillo.

Sandoval Family

Isaac Aragon Sandoval (May 22, 1862 to 1933). Commemorated with a stone. Husband of Victoria Sandoval. Isaac attended Billy's funeral.

Victoria G. Sandoval (1874 to December 15, 1916). Commemorated with a stone. Wife of Isaac Sandoval.

Celestino Sandoval (May 19, 1867 to December 2, 1950). Commemorated with a stone. Son of Isaac Sandoval.

> *"Celestino Sandoval of Fort Sumner died Dec. 1 at Fort Sumner. He was 83."*

> *"A justice of the peace there for many years, he is survived by his wife Margarita and five daughters. Burial took place at Old Fort Cemetery near Fort Sumner."* [31]

Rumalda Sandoval (May, 1886 to ??). Daughter of Isaac Sandoval.

Jose Ines Sandoval (1860 to ??).

Teodorita Sandoval (1890 to ??).

Silva Family

Jesus Maria Silva (October 13, 1853 to May 30, 1941). Commemorated with a stone. Jesus was Lucien Maxwell's ranch manager at Fort Sumner, and he continued in that position with Pete Maxwell after Lucien died.

> *"Jesus Maria Silva, 87, a pioneer of Billy the Kid days at Ft. Sumner, died Friday night at the home of his daughter-in-law, Mrs. Frank Silva, in the river town...."*

> *"Silva was born Oct. 13, 1853, at Bernalillo, and went to Ft. Sumner when he was 20 years old...."*

> *"Silva told of helping remove the Kid's body to a carpenter shop nearby where they placed the body on a carpenter's bench. There it was dressed for burial the next morning, he said."*

106 ~ Chapter 3

"Silva, blind at the end, had a vivid memory of those colorful days of the early 80s at Ft. Sumner. At that time he was a young man of prominence in his community and his acquaintanceship with the Kid and the latter's life was unquestioned by those who wrote of the Kid's wild exploits." [32]

Jesus was at Fort Sumner when O'Folliard was killed.

Mariana Spitz Silva (1855 to March 16, 1934). Wife of Jesus Silva.

"Mrs. Jesus Silva, age 79, wife of Jesus Silva, Sr., died Wednesday afternoon at 3:30 after an illness that had confined her to her bed for nearly two years, and was laid to rest Thursday afternoon in the Old Town cemetery." [33]

Maggie S. Silva (January 1, 1896, May 18, 1922). Commemorated with a stone. Daughter of Jesus Silva.

Luciano "Chano" Frank Silva (December 20, 1918 to May 26, 2004). Commemorated with a stone. Son of Jesus Silva. Luciano is the last person that will buried in the cemetery. To be buried there, he was forced to obtain a court order. The order permitted his burial, but forbid any additional burials.

Anaya Family

Jesus Anaya (1830 to ??). Father of A. P. "Paco" Anaya. Was at Fort Sumner when Billy was killed.

Gregorita Anaya (??).

Baca Family

Maria Baca (??).

Lucia Baca (??).

Beneranda Baca (??).

Coldoveo Baca (??).

Gallegos Family

Alejandro Gallegos (1850 to ??).

Francisco Gallegos (??).

Lobato [Lovato] Family

Pascual Lobato (1840 to ??).

Leandre Lobato (??).

Leandro Lobato (1878 to ??).

Madrid Family

Santos Madrid (born 1831 to ??). Husband of Anamaria Madrid.

Anamaria Madrid (1836 to ??). Wife of Santos Madrid.

Cemetery Burials ~ 107

Mares Family

Matilda Mares (February, 1885 to ??). Father was Anastacio Mares.

Juan Mares (??).

Cruz Mares (??).

Eziquiel Mares (??).

Pena Family

Adolfo Pena (??).

Tomas Pena (??).

Salguero Family

Pablo Salguero (1904 to ??).

Maria Salguero (??).

Trinidad Salguero (1895 to ??).

Segura Family

Telesfor Segura (1877 to ??). Son of Alejandro Segura, who served on Billy the Kid's coroner's jury. Brother to Abrana Garcia, possible girlfriend of Billy the Kid.

Eudalda Segura (??).

Amelia Segura (??).

Placita Segura (1889 to ??). Wife of Cresenciano Segura.

Cosme Segura (1873 to ??).

Velasquez Family

Antonio Velasquez (??).

Ramon Velasquez (??).

Zamora Family

Catarino Zamora (??).

Manuella Zamora (??).

Other Burials

Juan Alamendarez (1857 to ??)

Teresita Allala (??)

Juan Andres (??)

Candido Campbell (1883 to ??)

Maria Encinias (1855 to ??)

John Farris (1845 to December 29, 1879).

"In a shooting affray at Fort Sumner on the 29th ultimo John Farris was shot and killed by Barney Mason. Farris shot three times at Mason without any provocation, when the latter went off, got a pistol and returning to the store where Farris was, shot him twice in the breast." [34]

Juanita Martinez Garrett (?? to November, 1879). Married Pat Garrett in November, 1879. Juanita died within days of the marriage, after becoming violently ill during the marriage celebration.

"FORT SUMNER - Yellowed old burial records held by Justice of the Peace Celestino Sandoval Tuesday disclosed that lost somewhere in the half acre burial ground that holds the body of Billy the Kid is the grave of Juanita Garrett, first wife of Sheriff Pat Garrett who ended the Kid's bloody career with a blazing revolver in 1881." [35]

Juanita's sister was Celsa (Martinez) Gutierrez, possible girlfriend of Billy the Kid.

Joe Grant (?? to January 10, 1880). Commemorated by a wooden marker. Killed by Billy the Kid at Fort Sumner.

The only newspaper accounts of this killing are brief:

"Jan. 10; The "Kid" shot and killed Joe Grant, at Fort Sumner." [36]

"Billy Bonny, more extensively known as "the Kid," shot and killed Joe Grant. The origin of the difficulty was not learned." [37]

Second-hand accounts relate that the event occurred in the Hargrove Saloon at Fort Sumner. Grant was "viciously drunk" and had previously bragged that he was going to kill Billy. Billy apparently was aware of Grant's threat. After some talk, Billy asked to see Grant's revolver, saying he admired its "beauty." Before returning it, Billy secretly spun the pistol's cylinder so that the "next action would be a failure," being positioned on an empty chamber. After some more conversation, Grant turned his pistol on Billy and:

"...pulled the trigger, but the empty chamber refused to respond; with an oath [Grant] again raised the hammer, when a ball from the Kid's revolver crashed through his brains...." [38]

Isidro [Ysidro] Griego (1818 to ??)

Anastacio Indelecia (??)

Marcos Jaso (??)

George Lee (1878 to ??). Commemorated with a stone. Only the broken base of the marker remains.

John B. Legg (October 7, 1864 to March 22, 1899).

"John B. Legg, a well known character along the Rio Pecos, former deputy United States marshal, and for some years in the saloon business at Fort Sumner, was shot and killed at the latter place last week. Young James Blanton, aged

19, son of Capt. David Blanton, fired the fatal shot. It is claimed that he acted in self-defense. It appears that there had for some time been a feud between the two parties and in a course of a private conversation early in the evening the young man "roasted" Legg in rather severe terms. Later they met and Legg fired two shots, whereupon Blanton returned the fire and Legg fell, mortally wounded. He lived only a few hours."

"John B. Legg is known all over New Mexico and Texas. As an officer he was a fearless and trustworthy man...." [39]

Francisco "Frank" Medina (1856 to ??)

Antonia Molina (??)

Juan Montoya (1845 to ??)

Joseph Nalda (June 26, 1937 to June 30, 1938). Commemorated with a stone.

Nora Otero (??)

Juan Pacheco (??)

Christian Palmer (December 10, 1900 to July 3, 1902). Commemorated with a stone.

Elauteria Potter (??)

William "Willie" Florencio Spitz (July 21, 1858 to February 19, 1900).

Maria Trujillo (1855 to ??). Wife of Cruz Trujillo, who attended Billy the Kid's funeral.

Enriquez Valdez (??)

Reyes Wilcox (??)

Note: The author welcomes any additional information readers may have on the individuals buried in Fort Sumner.

110 ~ Chapter 3

Photos

Stone marker assigned to Marcus Cruiz, Pvt., 1st N.M. Cavalry, in the Sante Fe National Cemetery. Pvt. Cruiz died of intermittent fever, October 5, 1864. Pvt. Cruiz was one of 22 men moved from the Fort Sumner Cemetery to the Santa Fe National Cemetery on March 8, 1906.

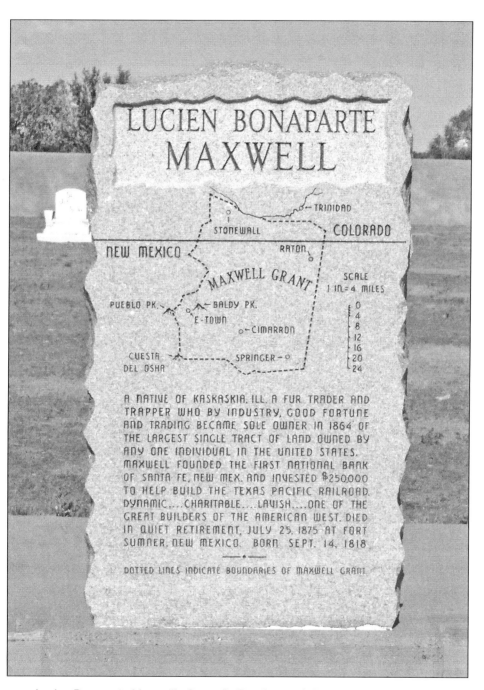

Lucien Bonaparte Maxwell's Grave (in Fort Sumner). To ensure a legal right to install the monument, the Fort Sumner Rotary Club purchased the grave from Lucien's living relatives. The monument was donated by Roy Erickson of the Denver Monument Company and designed by Wayne D. Gordon.

Lucien Bonaparte Maxwell. Born September 14, 1818, in Kaskaskia, Illinois. Died July 25, 1875, at Fort Sumner. Courtesy Arthur Johnson Memorial Library.

María de la Luz Beaubien Maxwell. Born June 28, 1829, in Taos, New Mexico. Died July 13, 1900, at Fort Sumner. Commemorated on the Abreu family stone. Married Lucien Maxwell on June 2, 1844. Courtesy Arthur Johnson Memorial Library.

Paulita (Paula) Maxwell. Born January, 1864, in Cimarron, New Mexico. Died December 17, 1929, at Fort Sumner. Commemorated on the Abreu family stone. Paulita married José Francisco Jaramillo on January 14, 1882. Courtesy Arthur Johnson Memorial Library.

Odile Bernice Maxwell. Born July 25, 1868, in Cimarron, New Mexico. Died May 5, 1935, at Fort Sumner. Commemorated on the Abreu family stone. She became Manuel Fernando Abreu's second wife on August 16, 1887. Courtesy Arthur Johnson Memorial Library.

116 ~ Chapter 3

The graves of Pete and Lucien Maxwell. The fence and wall surrounding Pete's grave were built by Charlie Foor. The rocks in the wall were taken from the fireplace in Pete's bedroom where Billy the Kid was shot. These rocks are the only things that remain of the Maxwell residence at Fort Sumner.

Cemetery Burials ~ 117

Pete Maxwell's gravestone. The stone has been chipped by souvenir hunters.

Joint gravestone for William Henry McCarty (alias William H. Bonney, alias William Antrim, alias Billy the Kid), Thomas O'Folliard, Jr., and Charles Meriwether Bowdre. The marker was erected in February, 1931.

Cemetery Burials ~ 119

The grave of Billy the Kid, Thomas O'Folliard, Jr., and Charles Meriwether Bowdre.

120 ~ Chapter 3

The barred cage protecting the gravestone of Billy the Kid, Thomas O'Folliard, Jr., and Charles Meriwether Bowdre.

The marker erected at the base of Billy's grave. The marker was donated by John N. Warner and installed on March 23, 1940. It has been stolen twice: once on August 29, 1950, and again on February 1, 1981. The first time the marker was missing for 26 years, the second time for 16 days.

Pablo C. Beaubien (August 24, 1849 to 1903). Married Rebecca Abreu Beaubien on August 6, 1870. Pablo was in Fort Sumner when Billy was killed and saw the body. Courtesy Arthur Johnson Memorial Library.

Gravestone for Pablo C. Beaubien. The remains of an earlier cement marker are still visible.

Rebecca Abreu Beaubien (August, 1855 to 1932) and unidentified daughter. Wife of Pablo C. Beaubien. Rebecca was in Fort Sumner when Billy was killed and saw the body. Courtesy Arthur Johnson Memorial Library.

Gravestone for Rebecca Abreu Beaubien.

Gravestones of Charles Wesley and Silberia Beaubien Foor. They were married October 29, 1884. Silberia was a Native American who was adopted while a young girl by Juan Christobal Beaubien and Maria Albina Beaubien.

Cemetery Burials ~ 127

Graves of Jesus Maria Silva (October 13, 1853 to May 30, 1941), Maggie S. Silva (January 1, 1896, May 18, 1922), and Luciano "Chano" Frank Silva (December 20, 1918 to May 26, 2004). Jesus Silva was the chief pallbearer at Billy's funeral.

Plaque on gravestone of Luciano "Chano" Frank Silva. Luciano Silva is the last person that will buried in the cemetery. To be buried there, he was forced to obtain a court order. The order permitted his burial, but forbid any additional burials.

Appendix A | Dudrow Correspondence

Sunny Side, N. M.
Feb. 21, 1906

Col. K. B. West,
Denver, Colo.

Dear Sir:

I herewith make report of disinterments at old Post Cemetery, Fort Sumner, N.M. as follows:

From information gathered from old residents of this part of the country I experienced no difficulty in locating the remains of all the officers and men as per list furnished and herewith returned. I have, however, been unable to identify the remains of each with but one exception. Some of the graves still had head boards but it was impossible to decipher any of them on account of their age as they were all made from pine and the lettering practically obliterated. Some of these head boards had rotted off at the ground and have been used to mark the graves of parties buried in recent years and in other parts of the cemetery.

I went to considerable trouble to hunt up all the old residents who might give me information which would enable me to identify the remains but have been unable to find a single old settler who could remember the name or locate the grave of any particular officer or man, although several were positive of the part of the cemetery used by the military. The exception mentioned above was in the case of the remains of Lieut. Wm. J. Eckley who I am positive of on account of the shoulder straps which were in a good state of preservation and showed him to have been a Second Lieutenant of Infantry, the only lieutenant in the list furnished. In the case of the two Captains there remained enough of the uniforms to show that they were buried in full dress, although the buttons were so corroded that it was impossible to distinguish any lettering. The shoulder straps worn by both showed them to be Cavalry Officers. The remains of Captain marked No. 18, were buried in a metal lined casket and at one time had quite an elaborate monument made of wood which was also quite well preserved, but all marks and lettering entirely obliterated. No. 8 proved to be a Corporal of Cavalry and was evidently an old man and had several re-enlistment stripes. With these exceptions there was nothing to identify any of the others. The remains of each and every one were in a fine state of preservation and the entire skeleton of every one secured. The bones were dry and clean and no odor noticed except in one instance and then only very slightly.

I enclose a rough drawing of the cemetery showing the approximate location of each grave and numbered right to left to correspond with the numbers of the boxes containing these bodies, trusting that this may be of some assistance in identifying these officers and men from your records.

From the information I have been able to gather I believe that the burials were made from right to left and probably follow in rotation according to date except in the case of the officers.

The remains will reach Santa Rosa about Feb. 28th where I have made arrangements with Mr. Frank Shane to store same until Bills of Lading can be issued by your office covering shipment to Santa Fe. This arrangement was made as the Railroad Agent at Santa Rosa informed me that on account of inadequate station facilities he could not hold remains until bills could reach him.

Following I give list of boxes by number and weight of each.

Very respectfully,
C. W. Dudrow

* * * * * * *

March 10, 1906

Col. C. A. H. McCauley,
A. Q. M. General U. S. A.
Denver, Colo.

Dear Sirs:

I am in receipt of copy of report of Austin J. Chapman, Supt. Of the U. S. National Cemetery of this place relative to the disinterment and removal of the remains of twenty-two officers and men from the old Post Cemetery at Ft. Sumner, also your request for report touching the matter referred to.

There are still interred in this cemetery probably from sixty to eighty persons, several having been interred within the last three or four years, and some of whom have relatives living at Ft. Sumner and vicinity. Among these are included the child of Maj. [Alexander Scammel Brooks] Keyes and four other children interred near where the soldiers were interred; also Lucien B. Maxwell one of the original owners of the Maxwell Land Grant, Peter Maxwell and two of his family, Billy the Kid, the notorious outlaw, and two of his gang and a number of others who it would be impossible to identify.

My understanding of the contract was the removal of all officers, men and civilian employees of the Army and my reason for not taking up the remains of Maj. Keyes child was that there are relatives living at Fort Sumner and it is the desire of these people to retain this plat for burial purposes if the ground can be secured from the government.

The reason for not disinterring the others was that I was under the impression that only persons belonging to or connected with the Army or Navy were permitted burial in a National Cemetery.

If the Quartermaster's Department construes this contract to cover the removal of all persons interred at old Post Cemetery, Ft. Sumner, upon notification of such fact I will proceed at once to complete the work. In this connection, however, I would ask instructions in case persons having relative interred in the old cemetery object to the removal of the remains what course shold (sic) be pursued.

Yours respectfully,
C. W. Dudrow

* * * * * * *

April 20, 1906

Col. C. A. H. McCauley,
A. Q. M. General U. S. A.

Dear Sirs:

I am in receipt of copy of letter of April 14th from Chief Quartermaster General referring to the removal of remains of soldiers from old post Cemetery at Fort Sumner to Santa Fe, N. M.

My original report of which I enclose copy, together with enclosed drawing of the cemetery I think practically covers the questions referred to.

As stated in that report it was impossible to identify the remains of any particular person. I spent five or six days traveling through the country in search of old residents who might be able to identify some one or more of these soldiers, but after the lapse of forty years it could hardly be considered possible to get reliable information as most of the old timers are dead and in a thinly settle country, such as this is, not much attention is paid to such matters. I had an interview with a Dr. John Gayhart [Gerhardt] whom I traveled fifty miles to see who was a caterer for the officers (sic) mess during the time of the post but he could remember nothing regarding names of anything of that nature. He was, however, able to tell me the part of the cemetery used by the military. He also told me about the wooden monument over the remains of one of Captains but could not recall the name. I also found other parties who gave practically the same information. At one time, so I was informed, all the graves of the soldiers were marked with wooden head boards and when I did this work some of them were still standing in the first and second rows but all lettering entirely obliterated and not even legible under a magnifying glass.

Referring to the apparent discrepancy regarding the identification of "No. 8, List Furnished" will say that in my report I did not assume to identify these remains by name. No. 8, as shown by enclosed drawing was a Corporal of Cavalry which was apparent when the grave was opened as the re-enlistment stripes on the sleeve were visible for probably a minute before the color and material crumbled away from exposure to the air.

The identification of the officers was made from the shoulder straps and clothing. The list furnished me giving the names of these twenty two officers and men contained but on Lieutenant consequently I am thouroughly (sic) convinced that there can be no mistake as to these remains being those of Wm. J. Eckley as the Second Lieutenant Shoulder straps would indicate, and the other two officers being Captains.

As shown by the drawing the graves of the three officers were close together. No. 18, was the one burried (sic) in a metalic (sic) casket and over whose grave was the large wooden monument. From the position of the grave, date of death, and black trowsers (sic) without stripes, found in this grave I am inclined to believe that this was the grave of Capt. Lusby, but there can be no certainty as to this on account of lack of reliable information. From information received from several parties I am satisfied that the interments were made from right to left and in my opinion, it would be quite likely that the first officer to be buried should be in the center of the rows in the part of the cemetery used for military burials.

The identification of the remains removed was as certain as could be expected after the long lapse of time as signified by the remaining head boards which were all of the same pattern, the information gathered as to the part of the cemetery used by the soldiers and the finding of something of a military nature in nearly all of the graves. In nearly every grave with the exception of the three officers, I found parts of the old government woolen sock.

The boxes in which the remains were shipped were numbered to correspond with the numbers as shown on the drawing enclosed.

Trusting that this will prove satisfactory and assuring you that the information is as full as I can give, I am,

Very respectfully,
C. W. Dudrow

Source: Fort Sumner Cemetery File, RG92, National Archives and Records Administration.

Appendix B | Interview with Sheriff Pat Garrett

This interview with Sheriff Pat F. Garrett was published one week after Billy's death. (**Source:** *Santa Fe Daily New Mexican,* July 21, 1881.)

Garrett Exonerates Maxwell

There is a disposition on the part of a good many people to censure Pete Maxwell for harboring Billy the Kid, the finding and killing of the desperado in Maxwell's house having given rise to much talk on the subject. In the view of this state of affairs a reporter of the NEW MEXICAN had a talk with Sheriff Garrett yesterday afternoon knowing that he would be more likely to know and more likely to tell the true state of things than almost anyone who could be found. Garret does not think that Maxwell was in with the Kid at all or that he deserves to be held responsible for the presence of the cutthroat in his house on the night upon which Billy met his death. He says that Pete was intimidated and was afraid to speak above a whisper when the Kid was around, otherwise he would have given notice of his whereabouts. Garrett knows Maxwell well and knows that this is in keeping with his disposition. He says that Pete acknowledged that fear kept him from informing on the Kid, and told him that if he could have found any safe way of letting Garrett know that this man was there he would have done so.

"How did the Kid happen to stop at Maxwell's house?" asked the reporter.

"He didn't stop there," replied Garrett. "He had only made three visits to Sumner since his escape and just came in unexpectedly while I was there. You see I went in to see Maxwell and ask him where the Kid was. I asked him as soon as I got in whether the Kid was in the country, and he became very much agitated, but answered that he was. Just then a man came in at the door and spoke to my men outside in Spanish, supposing them to be Mexicans. I didn't recognize him. He then came in and approached the bed, and after speaking to Maxwell, asked who were those outside. I had not had time to fix my revolver, and had not expected to see him there. I therefore reached around and adjusted it, and Maxwell started in the bed. The Kid pulled down on me, and asked 'Who is it?' He must have then recognized me, as I had him, for he went backward with a cat-like movement, and I jerked my gun and fired. The flash of the pistol blinded me, and I fired in the same direction again; and was ready to shoot the third time, but I heard him groan and knew he was struck. All this, however, has been told. What I want you to say, is, that Maxwell is not guilty of harboring the Kid."

"I shall do that, but I want to ask you a few questions first. How do you account for the Kid not shooting as soon as he recognized you?"

"I think he was surprised and thrown off his guard. Almost any man would have been. Kid was cool under trying circumstances as any man I ever saw. But he was so surprised and startled, that for a second he could not collect himself. Some men cannot recover their faculties for some time after such a shock. I think Kid would have done so in a second more, if he had had time."

134 ~ Appendix B

"It is said by some people that Kid was cowardly, and never gave a man a chance."

"No, he was game. I saw him give a man once. I have seen him tried. He would fight any way. I've known him to turn loose in a crowd of Mexicans, and get away with them. He would lick Mexicans that would weigh twenty-five or fifty pounds more than he did. He was quick as a flash."

"Was he a good shot?"

"Yes, but he was not better than the majority of men who are constantly handling and using six-shooters. He shot well, though, and he shot well under all circumstances, whether in danger or not."

"Why do you suppose he hung around Lincoln County, instead of leaving the country?"

"Oh, he thought that was his safest plan. In fact, he said so. He said that he was safer out on the plains, and could always get something to eat among the sheep herders. So he decided to take his chance out there where he was hard to get at."

After some more conversation, into which Mr. Garrett entered more freely than is his wont, and another reference to the Maxwell affair, the reporter left.

From the statements of all who know Pete Maxwell, it would appear that Garrett's idea is the correct one, and that he is guilty of nothing except of being abjectly afraid of the Kid.

Notes

1 – Introduction

1. Don Cline, *Antrim and Billy* (Creative Publishing Co., 1990), pp 44-47.

2. Cline, *Antrim and Billy,* p 49.

3. Cline, *Antrim and Billy,* p 59.

4. *Mining Life,* September 19, 1874.

5. *The Grant County Herald,* September 26, 1875. "Celestials" was common slang then for Chinese. "Sans Cue" means without a plaited hair braid. Joss sticks are incense sticks.

2 – Killing Billy – "Kid Talked Before He Shot"

1. William A. Keleher Papers, MSS 742 BC, Center for Southwest Research, University of New Mexico.

2. *The General Laws of New Mexico* (W. C. Little & Co, 1880), chapter LI, section 2, p 258.

3. William A. Keleher Papers, MSS 742 BC.

4. *Daily New Mexican,* April 15, 1881.

5. *Daily New Mexican,* April 16, 1881.

6. *Newman's Semi-Weekly,* April 20, 1881.

7. Pat F. Garrett, *The Authentic Life of Billy, the Kid, the Noted Desperado of the Southwest, Whose Deeds of Daring Have Made His Name a Terror in New Mexico, Arizona, and Northern Mexico* (University of Oklahoma Press, 1954), pp 132-133.

8. Eddie Taylor, "Eye Witness Prisoners: April 28, 1881," *The Outlaw Gazette,* November 2001, Vol. 14, p 18. The five other prisoners were Marejildo Torres, John Copeland, Augustin Davalas, Alexander Nunnelly, and Charles Wall

9. Garrett, *Authentic Life,* p 132.

10. Garrett, *Authentic Life,* p 133. Billy did mot kill James Carlyle, although he was present when Carlyle was killed.

11. Garrett, *Authentic Life,* p 134.

12. *Daily New Mexican,* April 20, 1881.

13. *Las Vegas Daily Optic,* May 3, 1881. Garrett, Authentic Life, p 140.

14. *Daily New Mexican,* May 3, 1881.

15. Garrett, *Authentic Life,* p 135.

16. *Daily New Mexican,* May 3, 1881.

17. *The New Southwest,* Supplement, May 14, 1881.

18. *Las Vegas Daily Gazette,* May 10, 1881.

19. *Tombstone Epitaph,* June 6, 1881.

20. *Lincoln County Leader,* March 1, 1890.

21. *Golden Era,* May 5, 1881.

22. *Lincoln County Leader,* March 1, 1890.

23. Garrett, *Authentic Life,* p 140.

24. Garrett, *Authentic Life,* pp 138-139.

25. Death Warrant of William Bonney, William A. Keleher Papers, MSS 742 BC.

26. Garrett, *Authentic Life,* pp 139-140.

27. *The New Southwest,* Supplement, May 14, 1881.

28. *Daily New Mexican,* June 16, 1881.

29. *Daily New Mexican,* May 5, 1881.

30. Garrett, Authentic Life, p 142.

31. *Daily New Mexican,* May 20, 1881.

32. John P. Wilson, *Fort Sumner, New Mexico* (Museum of New Mexico, 1974) pp 4-5.

33. Scott Smith, Letter to John Grassham, September 4, 1997, Library Files, Fort Sumner Bosque Redondo Memorial Monument.

34. Lawrence R. Murphy, *Lucien Bonaparte Maxwell* (University of Oklahoma Press, 1983), p 111. Don McAlavy, "Along the Pecos," manuscript, March, 1976, Fort Sumner Public Library.

35. Change of Venue Request, Territory of New Mexico vs William Bonney, alias Kid, alias William Antrim, April 21, 1879, Mary Daniels Taylor Papers, Archives and Special Collections, NMSU.

36. Lewis Wallace, Proclamation by the Governor, November 13, 1878, Lew Wallace Collection, M292 bx 3, fd 17, Indiana Historical Society.

37. Wallace, Proclamation by the Governor.

38. *Albuquerque Journal,* Nov 29, 1927. J. Evetts Haley, Interview with Deluvina Maxwell, June 24, 1927, Panhandle Plains Historical Museum Research Center.

39. *Dallas Morning News,* July 8, 1928.

40. J. Evetts Haley, Interview with Deluvina Maxwell, June 24, 1927.

41. Anaya, *I Buried Billy* (Creative Publishing Company, 1991), pp 75-76. Walter Noble Burns, *The Saga of Billy the Kid* (Grosset & Dunlap, 1926), p 186.

42. Anaya, *I Buried Billy,* p 77. Leon C. Metz, Pat Garrett, *The Story of a Western Lawman* (University of Oklahoma Press, 1974), p 58.

43. Marriage Registry, Anton Chico Catholic Church. Copy in author's possession.

44. John William Poe, *The Death of Billy the Kid* (Sunstone Press, 2006), pp 27-28.

45. 1880 Census for Fort Sumner, County of San Miguel, Territory of New Mexico, June 14, 1880, district 37, p 18.

46. Elbert A. Garcia, *Billy the Kid's Kid* (Los Products Press, 1999), pp 30, 32, 39.

47. 1880 Census for Fort Sumner, p 18.

48. Garcia, *Billy the Kid's Kid,* pp 38-39.

49. *Albuquerque Daily Journal,* July 18, 1881.

50. Burns, *The Saga of Billy the Kid,* pp 183-184.

51. Walter Noble Burns, "A Belle of Old Fort Sumner," manuscript chapter, Walter Noble Burns Papers, AZ 291, bx 1, fd 7, University of Arizona Special Collections, p 217.

52. Burns, "A Belle of Old Fort Sumner," p 219.

53. James W. Southwick, Letter to E. A. Brininstool, September 18, 1920, E. A. Brininstool Collection, bx 3g468, fd 2, Briscoe Center for American History, University of Texas at Austin.

54. James W. Southwick, Letter to E. A. Brininstool, September 25, 1920, E. A. Brininstool Collection, bx 3g468, fd 2, Briscoe Center for American History, University of Texas at Austin.

55. Burns, *The Saga of Billy the Kid,* pp 184.

56. Garrett, *Authentic Life,* p 143.

57. Garrett, *Authentic Life,* p 143.

58. Poe, *The Death of Billy the Kid,* pp 18-19.

59. Poe, *The Death of Billy the Kid,* pp 20-21.

60. Poe, *The Death of Billy the Kid,* p 23.

61. Poe, *The Death of Billy the Kid,* p 26.

62. Garrett, *Authentic Life,* p 144.

63. Poe, *The Death of Billy the Kid,* p 29.

64. Poe, *The Death of Billy the Kid,* p 28.

65. Garrett, *Authentic Life,* pp 144-145.

66. Poe, *The Death of Billy the Kid,* p 31.

67. Poe, *The Death of Billy the Kid,* p 31.

68. Poe, *The Death of Billy the Kid,* p 31.

69. *Las Vegas Gazette,* July 19, 1881.

70. *Las Vegas Gazette,* July 19, 1881.

71. *Rio Grande Republican,* July 23, 1881.

72. Poe, *The Death of Billy the Kid,* p 32.

73. Poe, *The Death of Billy the Kid,* pp 34-35.

74. *Rio Grande Republican,* July 23, 1881.

75. Poe, *The Death of Billy the Kid,* p 37.

76. Poe, *The Death of Billy the Kid,* p 37.

77. Poe, *The Death of Billy the Kid,* p 38.

78. Louis Leon Branch, *Los Bilitos: The Story of Billy the Kid and His Gang* (Carlton Press, 1980), p 251.

79. *Chicago Daily Tribune,* July 27, 1881. Anaya, I Buried Billy, pp 124-125, 127.

80. *Clovis Evening News Journal,* May 31, 1937. *Albuquerque Journal,* June 28, 1926.

81. Poe, *The Death of Billy the Kid,* p 40.

82. Garrett, *Authentic Life,* p 148.

83. Garrett, *Authentic Life,* pp 144-145.

84. Garrett, *Authentic Life,* p 145.

85. Garrett, *Authentic Life,* p 145.

86. Anaya, *I Buried Billy,* pp 124-125.

87. Anaya, *I Buried Billy,* p 125.

88. Anaya, *I Buried Billy,* p 126.

89. *Las Vegas Gazette,* July 19, 1881.

90. *Las Vegas Gazette,* July 19, 1881.

91. Garcia, *Billy the Kid's Kid,* p 33.

92. Garrett, *Authentic Life,* pp 151-152.

Notes ~ 137

93. Garrett, *Authentic Life,* p 148.

94. Poe, *The Death of Billy the Kid,* p 44.

95. *Clovis News-Journal,* July 13, 1938.

96. *Clovis News-Journal,* July 13, 1938.

97. *Rio Grande Republican,* July 23, 1881.

98. Coroner's Jury Report on William Bonney, July 15, 1881, Lincoln County Records, New Mexico State Records Center and Archives.

99. Coroner's Jury Report on William Bonney, July 15, 1881.

100. *Daily New Mexican,* May 5, 1881.

101. *Daily New Mexican,* July 21, 1881.

102. *Golden Era,* July 21, 1881.

103. *Daily New Mexican,* July 21, 1881.

104. *Rio Grande Republican,* July 23, 1881

105. *Las Vegas Daily Optic,* July 19, 1881.

106. *Rio Grande Republican,* July 23, 1881.

107. *Daily New Mexican,* July 21, 1881.

108. Act For the Relief of Pat Garrett, July 18, 1882, Territorial Auditor Papers, New Mexico State Records Center and Archives.

109. *The Roanoke Times,* December 14, 1892.

110. Fred R. Schwartzberg, "Pat Garrett Badge Authentication," *The Outlaw Gazette,* November, 2001, Vol. 14, p 17.

111. Poe, *The Death of Billy the Kid,* p 47.

112. *London Times,* August 18, 1881.

113. *Grant County Herald,* July 28, 1881.

114. *Santa Fe Weekly Democrat,* July 21, 1881.

115. *Las Vegas Daily Optic,* July 18, 1881

116. *Lincoln County Leader,* undated clipping.

117. *Lincoln County Leader,* undated clipping.

118. *Rio Grande Republican,* December 3, 1881.

119. *Rio Grande Republican,* April 8, 1882.

120. *Rio Grande Republican,* April 8, 1882.

121. *Las Vegas Daily Optic,* March 22, 1882.

2 – Billy's Grave - "The Bivouac of the Dead"

1. Robert M. McDonald, Letter to H. M. Enos, March 20, 1867, Fort Sumner Cemetery File, RG92, National Archives and Records Administration.

2. Coroner's Jury Report on William Bonney, July 15, 1881.

3. Anaya, *I Buried Billy,* p 132.

4. Anaya, *I Buried Billy,* p 132.

5. *Clovis News-Journal,* July 13, 1938.

6. Jean M. Burroughs, *On the Trail, The Life and Tales of "Lead Steer" Potter* (Museum of New Mexico Press, 1980), p 138. Evetts Haley, Interview with Deluvina Maxwell, June 24, 1927.

7. Burroughs, *On the Trail, The Life and Tales of "Lead Steer" Potter,* p 139.

8. *Clovis Evening News-Journal,* May 19, 1934.

9. *Las Vegas Daily Optic,* July 25, 1881.

10. *Las Vegas Daily Optic,* September 10, 1881.

11. *Las Vegas Daily Optic,* September 19, 1881.

12. *Las Vegas Daily Optic,* October 14, 1881.

13. Garrett, *Authentic Life,* p 149.

14. Poe, *The Death of Billy the Kid,* pp 46-47.

15. *Las Vegas Daily Optic,* March 13, 1891.

16. Burns, *The Saga of Billy the Kid,* p 189.

17. Burns, *The Saga of Billy the Kid,* p 193.

18. *Las Vegas Daily Optic,* January 16, 1882.

19. Don McAlavy, "Along the Pecos," March, 1976.

20. George B. Anderson, *History of New Mexico, Its Resources and People* (Pacific States Publishing Co., 1907) Vol 2, p 888.

21. *Las Vegas Daily Optic,* March 31, 1891.

22. *Albuquerque Citizen,* June 28, 1898.

23. *El Paso Herald,* August 31, 1901.

24. *The Philadelphia Times,* June 29, 1902.

25. *The Socorro Chieftain,* October 8, 1904.

26. Bob Parsons, *Living Water: Our Mid-Pecos History* (Mid-Pecos Historical Foundation, 1983), p 24.

27. *El Paso Herald,* October 10, 1905.

28. *El Paso Herald,* October 14, 1905.

29. *El Paso Herald,* December 9, 1905.

30. *Clovis Evening News-Journal,* May 19, 1934.

31. *Albuquerque Evening Citizen,* January 13, 1906.

32. *Albuquerque Evening Citizen,* December 15, 1905.

33. Charles W. Dudrow, Letter to Col. C. A. H. McCauley, March 10, 1906, Fort Sumner Cemetery File, RG92, National Archives and Records Administration.

34. *Albuquerque Evening Citizen,* January 13, 1906.

35. "Disinterring and Removing Remains of Officers, Enlisted Men and Civilians at Old Fort Sumner, New Mexico," December 2, 1905, B. K. West, Lt. Col. Deputy Commissary General, U.S.A, Fort Sumner Cemetery File, RG92, National Archives and Records Administration.

36. Charles W. Dudrow, Letter to Col. C. A. H. McCauley, April 20, 1906, Fort Sumner Cemetery File, RG92, National Archives and Records Administration.

37. Albuquerque Evening Citizen, March 3, 1906.

38. Charles W. Dudrow, Letter to Col. K. B. West, April 20, 1906, Fort Sumner Cemetery File, RG92, National Archives and Records Administration.

39. *Dallas Morning News,* July 8, 1928.

40. *Albuquerque Journal,* November 29, 1927.

41. *Albuquerque Journal,* Nov 28, 1927.

42. *Albuquerque Journal,* November 29, 1927.

43. *New Mexico State Tribune,* November 29, 1927.

44. Mark J. Dworkin, *American Mythmaker, Walter Noble Burns and the Legends of Billy the Kid, Wyatt Warp, and Joaquin Murrieta* (University of Oklahoma Press, 2015), pp 15, 18.

45. Dworkin, *American Mythmaker,* p 24.

46. *El Paso Herald,* June 5, 1926.

47. *El Paso Herald,* August 25, 1927.

48. *El Paso Herald,* June 5, 1926.

49. *El Paso Herald,* August 25, 1927.

50. *El Paso Herald,* October 15, 1928.

51. *The Fort Sumner Leader,* April 11, 1930

52. *Las Vegas Daily Optic,* January 24, 1933.

53. *Albuquerque Journal,* June 28, 1926.

54. *Clovis News-Journal,* July 13, 1938.

55. *Alamogordo News,* May 15, 1930. El Paso Herald, February 26, 1935.

56. *Clovis Evening News-Journal,* May 31, 1937.

57. *Alamogordo News,* May 15, 1930.

58. *Albuquerque Journal,* January 25, 1962.

59. *Alamogordo News,* July 3, 1930.

60. David G. Thomas, *Screen With A Voice, A History of Moving Pictures in Las Cruces, New Mexico* (Doc45 Publishing, 2016), pp 69, 76-77.

61. David G. Thomas, *Screen With A Voice,* p 77.

62. *Las Cruces Citizen,* October 25, 1930.

63. *Hope Star,* February 27, 1931.

64. *The Fort Sumner Leader,* October 31, 1930.

65. *Hope Star,* February 27, 1931.

66. *Roswell Daily Record,* July 22, 1932.

67. *Albuquerque Journal,* July 23, 1932.

68. *The Fort Sumner Leader,* October 14, 1932.

69. *Clovis Evening News-Journal,* May 31, 1937.

70. Manuel Abreu, F. W. Spitz, and Kenneth Miller vs. John W. Allen, Case 2184, February, 11, 1939, Tenth District Court, De Baca County, New Mexico.

71. *The Fort Sumner Leader,* July 8, 1938.

72. Clovis Evening News-Journal, March 30, 1931.

73. *Clovis News-Journal,* July 12, 1938.

74. *Clovis News-Journal,* July 24, 1938.

75. *New Mexico Sentinel,* Aug 14, 1938.

76. *New Mexico Sentinel,* Aug 14, 1938.

77. Manuel Abreu, F. W. Spitz, and Kenneth Miller vs. John W. Allen, Case 2184, February, 11, 1939.

78. Manuel Abreu, F. W. Spitz, and Kenneth Miller vs. John W. Allen, Case 2184, February, 11, 1939.

79. *Albuquerque Journal,* February 18, 1939.

Notes ~ 139

80. Manuel Abreu, F. W. Spitz, and Kenneth Miller vs. John W. Allen, Case 2184, February, 11, 1939.

81. Manuel Abreu, F. W. Spitz, and Kenneth Miller vs. John W. Allen, Case 2184, February, 11, 1939.

82. *Clovis News-Journal,* June 3, 1976.

83. *The Fort Sumner Leader,* March 26, 1940.

84. Clovis News-Journal, June 3, 1976.

85. *The Fort Sumner Leader,* March 26, 1940.

86. *The Fort Sumner Leader,* March 26, 1940.

87. *The Fort Sumner Leader,* March 26, 1940.

88. Albuquerque Journal, May 26, 1949.

89. *Clovis News Journal,* May 30, 1949.

90. *Clovis News-Journal,* May 26, 1949.

91. *Clovis News-Journal,* May 26, 1949.

92. *Albuquerque Journal,* August 30, 1950.

93. *Hobbs News-Sun,* April 24, 1961.

94. *Alamogordo Daily News,* April 27, 1961.

95. *El Paso Herald-Post,* May 3, 1961.

96. *Alamogordo Daily News,* June 1, 1961.

97. *El Paso Herald-Post,* May 31, 1961.

98. *Alamogordo Daily News,* June 1, 1961.

99. *Alamogordo Daily News,* June 1, 1961. George W. Coe, Frontier Fighter (R. R. Donnelley & Sons Co., 1984), p 228.

100. *Clovis News-Journal,* May 11, 1961.

101. *Albuquerque Journal,* May 6, 1961.

102. *Las Cruces Sun-News,* June 23, 1961.

103. *El Paso Herald-Post,* May 31, 1961.

104. *Clovis News-Journal,* May 7, 1945. *Independent* (Long Beach, CA), June 28, 1961.

105. *Alamogordo Daily News,* June 1, 1961.

106. *El Paso Herald-Post,* May 31, 1961.

107. *Las Vegas Daily Optic,* June 30, 1961.

108. *Clovis News-Journal,* July 19, 1961.

109. Application for the Removal of the Body of William H. Bonney, Deceased, from the Ft. Sumner Cemetery in which He Is Interred for Reinterment in the Lincoln, New Mexico, Cemetery, Case 3255, June 26, 1961, Tenth District Court, De Baca County, New Mexico.

110. *Clovis News-Journal,* July 28, 1961.

111. *Las Vegas Daily Optic,* November 16, 1961.

112. *Las Vegas Daily Optic,* November 16, 1961.

113. Las Vegas Daily Optic, November 16, 1961.

114. *Albuquerque Journal,* January 25, 1962.

115. *Albuquerque Journal,* January 25, 1962.

116. *Lubbock Avalanche-Journal,* March 13, 1962.

117. *De-Baca County-News,* March 15, 1962.

118. *Lubock Avalanche-Journal,* March 14, 1962.

119. *Lubock Avalanche-Journal,* March 14, 1962.

120. *Lubock Avalanche-Journal,* March 14, 1962.

121. *Lubock Avalanche-Journal,* March 14, 1962.

122. *Lubock Avalanche-Journal,* March 14, 1962.

123. *Albuquerque Journal,* June 30, 1973.

124. Clovis News-Journal, May 23, 1976.

125. *Clovis News-Journal,* May 23, 1976.

126. *Clovis News-Journal,* May 23, 1976.

127. *Clovis News-Journal,* May 23, 1976.

128. *Clovis News-Journal,* May 23, 1976.

129. *Las Cruces Sun-News,* May 21, 1976.

130. *De Baca County News,* Feb 5, 1981.

131. *Akron Beacon Journal* (Akron, OH), February 11, 1981.

132. *Albuquerque Journal,* Feb 14, 1981.

133. Scott Smith, Letter to Chris Roberts, August 28, 1999, Library Files, Fort Sumner Bosque Redondo Memorial Monument, quoted with the permission of the writer.

134. *Santa Fe New Mexican,* June 19, 1926.

135. *Des Moines Sunday Register,* September 19, 1926.

136. *El Paso Herald,* June 23, 1926.

137. *Des Moines Sunday Register,* September 19, 1926.

138. *Albuquerque Journal,* June 28, 1926.

140 ~ Notes

139. *Albuquerque Journal,* June 28, 1926.

140. *Albuquerque State Tribune,* June 27, 1926.

141. *Albuquerque State Tribune,* June 27, 1926.

142. *El Paso Herald,* June 26, 1926.

143. David G. Thomas, *Screen With A Voice,* p 102.

144. *Las Cruces Sun News,* March 9, 1947

3 – Cemetery Burials

1. *New Mexico Sentinel,* Aug 14, 1938. This is the primary source for the burials listed in this chapter.

2. *Las Vegas Daily Optic,* November 16, 1961.

3. Dan Scurlock, "Chano Silva Interview," January 13, 2000, manuscript, Fort Sumner Public Library.

4. *New Mexico Sentinel,* Aug 14, 1938.

5. Anaya, *I Buried Billy,* pp 75-76. Burns, *The Saga of Billy the Kid,* p 186.

6. 1880 Census for Fort Sumner, County of San Miguel, Territory of New Mexico, June 14, 1880, district 37, p 18.

7. Gregory Michno, *Encyclopedia of Indian Wars: Western Battles and Skirmishes, 1850-1890* (Mountain Press Pub. Co., 2003), p 203.

8. Record of Interments in the Post Cemetery at Fort Sumner, New Mexico, 1863 to 1868, Fort Sumner Cemetery File, RG92, National Archives and Records Administration.

9. Austin J. Chapman, Letter to Quartermaster, U. S. Army, Washington, D. C., March 8, 1906, Fort Sumner Cemetery File, RG92, National Archives and Records Administration.

10. Charles W. Dudrow, Map of Fort Sumner Cemetery, April 20, 1906, Fort Sumner Cemetery File, RG92, National Archives and Records Administration.

11. *Clovis News-Journal,* May 26, 1949.

12. *Las Vegas Gazette,* July 31, 1875.

13. *Albuquerque Citizen,* July 20, 1900.

14. *Clovis Evening News-Journal,* May 31, 1937.

15. *Weekly Optic and Stock Grower,* May 25, 1898.

16. *Albuquerque Citizen,* January 27, 1899.

17. *The Fort Sumner Review,* May 10, 1935.

18. *The Fort Sumner Leader,* December 20, 1929.

19. *Arizona Daily Sun* (Flagstaff, AZ), October 26, 1973.

20. Ralph Emerson Twitchell, *The Leading Facts of New Mexico History* (The Torch Press, 1917), Vol 3, pp 292-293.

21. *Clovis News-Journal,* March 31, 1940.

22. *Albuquerque Daily Citizen,* February 2, 1902.

23. *Albuquerque Daily Citizen,* March 6, 1902.

24. *Albuquerque Daily Citizen,* November 15, 1902.

25. *Albuquerque Morning Journal,* November 20, 1903.

26. *Albuquerque Morning Journal,* July 20, 1907.

27. *Clovis News-Journal,* January 4, 1940.

28. Anderson, *History of New Mexico, Its Resources and People,* p 888.

29. *The Fort Sumner Review,* April 6, 1918.

30. *Albuquerque Morning Journal,* May 12, 1912.

31. *Albuquerque Journal,* December 6, 1950.

32. *Clovis News-Journal,* June 1, 1941.

33. *The Fort Sumner Review,* March 16, 1934.

34. *Daily New Mexican,* December 29, 1879.

35. *New Mexico Sentinel,* Aug 14, 1938.

36. *Las Vegas Daily Gazette,* January 28, 1880.

37. *Santa Fe Weekly New Mexican,* January 17, 1880.

38. Garrett, *Authentic Life,* p 88.

39. *El Paso Daily Herald,* April 8, 1899.

Index

A

Abreu, Alfredo Napoleon, 101
Abreu, Amalia Mares, 102
Abreu, Enriques, 102
Abreu, Jesus L., 98, 102
Abreu, Luz Berenisa, 101
Abreu, Manuel Fernando, 11, 44, 57, 67, 95, 99, 101-102, 115
Abreu, Manuel Fernando, Jr., 101
Abreu, Pablo, 16
Alamendarez, Juan, 107
Allala, Teresita, 107
Allen, John W., 55-57, 61, 88, 90
Allen, John W., Mrs., 61, 63
Allen, Russell Paul, 129
Allen, S. E., 108
Anaya, A. P. "Paco," 16-17, 52-53, 65, 67, 81, 85, 87, 106
Anaya, Gregorita, 106
Anaya, Jesus, 106
Andres, Juan, 107
Antrim, William H., 1

B

Baca, Beneranda, 106
Baca, Coldoveo, 106
Baca, Lucia, 106
Baca, Maria, 106
Bail, John D., 3
Barrett, Louisa Beaubien, 57
Beaubien, Carlos, 97-98
Beaubien, Concepcion, 103
Beaubien, Felipe, 102
Beaubien, Juan Christobal, 102-103, 126
Beaubien, Maria Albina Trujillo, 102-103, 126
Beaubien, Pablo C., 16, 95, 102, 122-124
Beaubien, Paul C., 103
Beaubien, Rebecca Abreu, 16, 95, 102, 122, 124-125
Beaubien, Severo, 102
Beckwith, Bob, 4
Beery, Wallace, 53
Bell, James W., 4-7, 20
Bent, Charles, 98
Bernardo, Margaret Salazar, 61
Berney, Joseph, 96
Blanton, David, 109
Blanton, James, 108
Blazer, Joseph Hoy, 61
Blazer, Paul A., 61
Blythe, Dee, 55
Bonney, Orris, 60

Bonney, Thomas, 60
Bonney, William, 60-61
Bowdre, Charles Meriwether, 17, 41, 44, 46, 49, 51-55, 61, 63, 65, 70, 82, 85-86, 95, 100-101, 118-120
Bowdre, Frank, 63
Bowdre, George W., Sr., 63
Bowdre, Louis A., 61-63
Bowdre, Manuella, 17
Bowlin, Joe, 64
Brady, William, 3, 9, 12, 20, 60, 100
Branham, Mr. and Mrs., 63-64
Brazil, Manuel S., 13, 100-101
Bristol, Warren Henry, 3, 9, 23
Brown, Henry, 10
Brown, Johnny Mack, 53-54
Brunswick, M., 19
Burns, Walter Noble, 12, 50-51, 53, 66
Bursey, Joe, 59
Burt, Billy, 7, 22

C

Campbell, Candido, 107
Carlyle, James, 4
Carson, Kit, 98
Catron, T. B., 19
Chadderdon, W. S., 45
Chapman, Austin J., 130
Chase, C. C., Jr., 60-63
Chauncey, 47
Chavez, Juan, 96
Chung, Sam, 1
Clancy, Carlos F., 62
Coe, Frank, 60
Coe, George W., 61
Coe, Wilbur F., 60
Compton, J. C., 62
Cook, George, 103
Cook, James, 97
Coulter, Robert J., 61
Cruiz, Marcus, 96, 110
Crutchfield, Albertin, 96

D

Delaney, John C., 7
Deluvina Maxwell, 10, 11, 16, 32, 41, 49, 50, 52, 67, 72, 103
Devine, John, 97
Dolan, James J., 9, 19
Dougherty, William, 96
Dudrow, Charles W., 2, 48, 49, 65, 70, 96-97, 130, 132

142 ~ Index

E

Eckley, William J., 96-97, 129, 131
Edwards, William C., 96
Encinias, Maria, 107
Epple, William, 97
Erickson, Roy, 59, 97, 111
Essinger, Sophie, 63-64

F

Fairbanks, Douglas, 54
Farris, John, 44, 108
Foor, Charles Wesley, 50, 52-55, 65, 67, 76-77, 79-81, 85, 99, 102-103, 116
Foor, Silberia Beaubien, 99, 102-103, 126
Fountain, Albert J., 3, 20, 39
Friel, Hugh, 96

G

Gallegos, Alejandro, 106
Gallegos, Francisco, 106
Gallegos, J. V., 61
Gallegos, Judge, 62
Garcia, Abrana (Segura), 10-12, 16-17, 95, 103, 107
Garcia, Antonio, 103-104
Garcia, Francisca, 103
Garcia, Higinio, 16
Garcia, Isidora, 104
Garcia, Martin, 12, 16, 103
Garcia, Navora, 103-104
Garcia, Nipomocino, 103
Garcia, Ricardo, 103-104
Garcia, Reveca [Rebecca], 104
Garcia, Rose, 104
Gardiner, Leland V., 66, 68
Garrett, Elizabeth, 68
Garrett, Jarvis P., 64, 68
Garrett, Juanita Martinez, 10-11, 96, 108
Garrett, Oscar L., 68
Garrett, Patrick F., 2-5, 7-8, 10-11, 13-22, 25, 39-41, 43-48, 53, 55-56, 60, 62, 64, 66-68, 87, 100-101, 108, 133-134
Garrett, Pauline, 68
Gauss, Gottfried, 5-6, 30
Gerhardt, 48, 131
Gonzales, Jose J., 104
Gonzales, Juan N., 104
Gonzales, Juanita S., 104
Gonzales, Montoya, 104
Gonzales, Rumaldo, 104
Goodloe, Lori Ann, 39
Gordon, Wayne D., 59, 97, 111
Grant, Joe, 44, 105, 108
Griego, Isidro [Ysidro], 108
Gutierrez, Apolinaria, 11, 96, 101
Gutierrez, Celsa (Martinez), 10, 13, 96, 108
Gutierrez, Celsa, 11, 16-17
Gutierrez, Feliciana, 11

Gutierrez, Jose Dolores, 11, 96
Gutierrez, Mauricia, 11
Gutierrez, Sabal, 11, 16-18, 41, 96

H

Hale, L. W., 42
Harris, Arron Brown, 74-75, 104
Harris, Arron Brown, Jr., 104
Harris, Edward B., 104
Harris, Emma, 104
Hedgecook, Thomas, 97
Hensley, E. T., Jr., 62-63
Holzman, Philip, 102
Hough, Emerson, 45-48
Hughes, Howard, 68

I

Indelecia, Anastacio, 108

J

Jaramillo, Clemente, 105
Jaramillo, Jose Francisco, 16, 37, 95, 100, 105
Jaramillo, Lola (Dolores), 105
Jaramillo, Lorenzo, 16, 18, 95, 105
Jaso, Marcos, 108
Johnson, Edward, 97
Johnson, Patrick, 96
Julian, Walter F., 62, 95

K

Kerr, William, 97
Keyes, Alexander, 97, 130
Keyes, Virginia (Maxwell), 97

L

Lee, George, 108
Lee, John, 97
Legg, John B., 108-109
Leis, Henry, 36
Leonard, Ira E., 6
Lobato, Frank, 16, 57, 67
Lobato, Leandre, 106
Lobato, Leandro, 106
Lobato, Marie, 16
Lobato, Pascual, 106
Lopez, Joe, 26
Lucero, Alfredo, 57
Lucero, Pedro Antonio, 18
Lusby, Robert, 96, 131
Lutes, Sarah "Sadie" C., 99

M

Madrid, Anamaria, 106
Madrid, Santos, 106
Marcus, Juan, 96
Mares, Anastacio, 107

Index ~ 143

Mares, Cruz, 107
Mares, Eziquiel, 107
Mares, Juan, 107
Mares, Matilda, 107
Martinez, Albino, 10-11, 96
Martinez, Feliciana, 11
Mason, Barney, 44, 108
Massegee, George, 103
Maxwell, Emelia, 95, 99, 101
Maxwell, Julian, 100
Maxwell, Lavina, 67
Maxwell, Lucien Bonaparte, 9-10, 12, 35, 41, 45, 49, 57, 59, 67, 97-102, 104-105, 111-113, 116, 130
Maxwell, María de la Luz Beaubien, 16, 45, 95, 98-100, 102, 113
Maxwell, Odila Bernice (Abreu), 12, 16, 67, 95, 99, 100-101, 115
Maxwell, Paulita "Paula" (Jaramillo), 10, 12, 16, 37, 44, 50, 52, 67, 95, 100, 105, 114
Maxwell, Peter "Pete" Menard, 9-10, 12, 14-17, 18, 21, 36, 41, 44-46, 55, 50-52, 56, 67, 69, 76-77, 95, 99, 101, 105, 116-117, 130, 133-134
McCarty, Catherine, 1
McCarty, Joseph, 1
McCauley, C. A. H., 130-131
McDonald, Robert M., 41
McKinney, Thomas C. "Kip," 13-14, 16, 18, 20, 46
McSween, Alexander A., 9
Medina, Francisco "Frank," 67, 109
Medina, Juan, 67
Middleton, John, 10
Miller, George, 16
Miller, Kenneth, 57
Miranda, Guadalupe, 97
Molina, Antonia, 109
Montoya, Juan, 109
Murphy, Lawrence G., 9

N

Nalda, Joseph, 109
Narbono, Chief, 97
Neal, Whit, 103
Newcomb, Simon B., 3
Nickey, Billy, 7
Nicolson, Walter, 64-65

O

O'Folliard, Thomas "Tom", Jr., 41, 44, 46, 49, 5-55, 61, 65, 70, 82, 85-86, 95, 100, 106, 118-120
Olinger, Robert, 4-7, 20, 29
Otero, 52-53, 65, 85
Otero, Miguel A., Sr., 67
Otero, Nora, 109
Otero, Vincente, 16, 41, 67, 81
Owen, Richard, 98

P

Pacheco, Juan, 109
Page, Frank N., 44
Palmer, Christian, 109
Patton, Harry L., 57
Pena, Adolfo, 107
Pena, Tomas, 107
Perkins, J. T., 52, 62, 82, 100
Perry, Mayme Coe, 61
Phelps, William Lyon, 47
Pickett, Thomas "Tom", 17, 100-101
Poe, John William, 11-16, 18, 20, 33, 43, 46, 50
Potter, Elauteria, 109
Potter, Jack, 47, 69

R

Redin, Padre, 21
Rey, 80
Rhodes, Allen, 61
Rhodes, Eugene Manlove, 61
Ritch, William G., 19
Roberts, Buckshot, 61
Rudabaugh, Dave, 17, 100-101
Rudulph, Milnor, 13-14, 18, 38
Rynerson, William L., 9

S

Saavedra, Antonio, 18
Salazar, Yginio, 8, 31, 50, 61
Salguero, Maria, 107
Salguero, Pablo, 107
Salguero, Trinidad, 107
Sandoval, Celestino, 57, 105, 108
Sandoval, Isaac Aragon, 16, 95, 105
Sandoval, Jose Ines, 105
Sandoval, Rumalda, 105
Sandoval, Teodorita, 105
Sandoval, Victoria G., 105
Savadera, Antonio, 41
Segura, Alejandro, 11, 18, 107
Segura, Amelia, 107
Segura, Cosme, 107
Segura, Cresenciano, 107
Segura, Eudalda, 107
Segura, Fernando, 103
Segura, Fernando, 11
Segura, Manuel, 103
Segura, Manuel, 11
Segura, Telesfor, 107
Shaffer, George "Sombrero Jack", 1
Silva, Frank, Mrs., 105
Silva, Jesus Maria, 16-18, 41, 52-53, 62, 65, 78, 81, 85, 95, 105-106, 127
Silva, Jose, 18

144 ~ Index

Silva, Luciano "Chano" Frank, 62, 95, 106, 127-128
Silva, Maggie S., 106, 127
Silva, Mariana Spitz, 106
Smith, John, 103
Smith, Scott, 65
Southwick, James W., 12
Spitz, F. W., 57
Spitz, William "Willie" Florencio, 109
St. Vrain, Ceran, 98
Stahl, Robert J., 68
Stout, J. H., 98
Strunk, Samuel, 96
Sumner, Edwin Vose, 8
Sun, Charley, 1
Surbacker, D., 67
Sutton, Fred E., 49
Sweet, Tim, 94

T

Taylor, Manuel, 66, 68
Telfer, Lois H., 60-63
Tenney, Kate, 43
Tingley, Clyde, 56-57
Toury, Patrick, 96
Trujillo, Cruz, 67, 109
Trujillo, Maria, 109
Trujillo, Santion, 67
Tunstall, John Henry, 9

V

Valdez, Enriquez, 109
Velasquez, Antonio, 107
Velasquez, Ramon, 107
Vidor, King, 53

W

Wade, James F., 99
Waite, Fred, 10
Wallace, Lewis "Lew," 7-10, 18-20, 24, 45
Warner, John N., 58, 63-64, 92, 100, 121
Welbourn, Adelina J., 57, 59
Welbourn, Adelina J., Mrs., 88
Welsh, Philip, 96
Wesley, Charles, 126
West, K. B., 129
White, Edward, 97
Wilcox, Reyes, 109
Wilcox, Thomas, 101
Wilson, Billy, 17, 100-101
Wright, Gaylan. 64

Z

Zamora, Catarino, 107
Zamora, Manuella, 107

Index ~ 145

Joint gravestone for William Henry McCarty (alias William H. Bonney, alias William Antrim, alias Billy the Kid), Thomas O'Folliard, Jr., and Charles Meriwether Bowdre. The marker was erected in February, 1931.

Doc45 Publications

La Posta – From the Founding of Mesilla, to Corn Exchange Hotel, to Billy the Kid Museum, to Famous Landmark, David G. Thomas, paperback, 118 pages, 59 photos, e-book available.

"For someone who grew up in the area of Mesilla, it's nice to have a well-researched book about the area – and the giant photographs don't hurt either.... And the thing I was most excited to see is a photo of the hotel registry where the name of "William Bonney" is scrawled on the page.... There is some debate as to whether or not Billy the Kid really signed the book, which the author goes into, but what would Billy the Kid history be without a little controversy?" –Billy the Kid Outlaw Gang Newsletter, Winter, 2013.

Giovanni Maria de Agostini, Wonder of The Century – The Astonishing World Traveler Who Was A Hermit, David G. Thomas, paperback, 208 pages, 59 photos, 19 maps, e-book available.

"David G. Thomas has finally pulled back the veil of obscurity that long shrouded one of the most enduring mysteries in New Mexico's long history to reveal the true story of the Hermit, Giovanni Maria de Agostini. ...Thomas has once again proven himself a master history detective. Of particular interest is the information about the Hermit's life in Brazil, which closely parallels his remarkable experience in New Mexico, and required extensive research in Portuguese sources. Thomas's efforts make it possible to understand this deeply religious man." – Rick Hendricks, New Mexico State Historian

Screen With A Voice - A History of Moving Pictures in Las Cruces, New Mexico, David G. Thomas, paperback, 194 pages, 102 photos, e-book available.

The first projected moving pictures were shown in Las Cruces 110 years ago. Who exhibited those movies? What movies were shown? Since projected moving pictures were invented in 1896, why did it take ten years for the first movie exhibition to reach Las Cruces? Who opened the first theater in town? Where was it located? These questions began the history of moving pictures in Las Cruces, and they are answered in this book. But so are the events and stories that follow.

There have been 21 movie theaters in Las Cruces – all but three or four are forgotten. They are unremembered no longer. And one, especially, the Airdome Theater which opened in 1914, deserves to be known by all movie historians – it was an automobile drive-in theater, the invention of the concept, two decades before movie history declares the drive-in was invented.

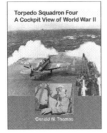

Torpedo Squadron Four – A Cockpit View of World War II, Gerald W. Thomas, paperback, 280 pages, 209 photos, e-book available.

"This book contains more first-person accounts than I have seen in several years. ...we can feel the emotion... tempered by the daily losses that characterized this final stage of the war in the Pacific. All in all, one of the best books on the Pacific War I have seen lately." – Naval Aviation News, Fall 2011.

Killing Pat Garrett, The Wild West's Most Famous Lawman - Murder or Self-Defense?

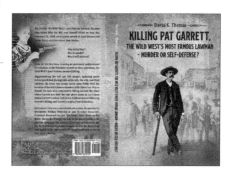

Pat Garrett, the Wild West's most famous lawman – the man who killed Billy the Kid – was himself killed on leap day, February 29, 1908, on a barren stretch of road between his Home Ranch and Las Cruces, New Mexico.

> Who killed him?
> Was it murder?
> Was it self-defense?

No biographer of Garrett has been able to answer these questions. All have expressed opinions. None have presented evidence that would stand up in a court of law. Here, for the first time, drawing on newly discovered information, is the definitive answer to the Wild West's most famous unsolved killing.

Supplementing the text are 102 images, including six of Garrett and his family which have never been published before. It has been 50 years since a new photo of Garrett was published, and no photos of his children have ever been published.

Garrett's life has been extensively researched. Yet, the author was able to uncover an enormous amount of new information. He had access to over 80 letters that Garrett wrote to his wife. He discovered a multitude of new documents and details concerning Garrett's killing, the events surrounding it, and the personal life of the man who was placed on trial for killing Garrett.

- The true actions of "Deacon Jim" Miller, a professional killer, who was in Las Cruces the day Garrett was killed.
- The place on the now abandoned old road to Las Cruces where Garrett was killed.
- The coroner's jury report on Garrett's death, lost for over 100 years.
- Garrett's original burial location.
- The sworn courtroom testimony of the only witness to Garrett's killing.
- The policeman who provided the decisive evidence in the trial of the man accused of murdering Garrett.
- The location of Garrett's Rock House and Home Ranches.
- New family details: Garrett had a four-month-old daughter the day he killed Billy the Kid. She died tragically at 15. Another daughter was blinded by a well-intended eye treatment; a son was paralyzed by childhood polio; and Pat Garrett, Jr., named after his father, lost his right leg to amputation at age 12.

Garrett's life was a remarkable adventure. He met two United States presidents: President William McKinley, Jr. and President Theodore Roosevelt. President Roosevelt he met five times, three times in the White House. He brought the law to hardened gunmen. He oversaw hangings. His national fame was so extensive the day he died that newspapers from the East to the West Coast only had to write "Pat Garrett" for readers to know to whom they were referring.

2019 Best Book Awards Finalist, United States History
2019 Best Indie Book Notable 100 Award Winner.
2019 Royal Dragonfly Book Award Winner, Second Place, Historical Non-Fiction

The Stolen Pinkerton Reports of the Colonel Albert J. Fountain Murder Investigation, David G. Thomas, Editor, paperback, 194 pages, 28 photos.

The abduction and apparent murder of Colonel Albert J. and Henry Fountain on February 1, 1896, shocked and outraged the citizens of New Mexico. It was not the killing of Colonel Fountain, a Union Civil War veteran and a prominent New Mexico attorney, which roused the physical disgust of the citizenry - after all, it was not unknown for distinguished men to be killed. It was the cold-blooded murder of his eight-year-old son which provoked the public outcry and revulsion.

The evidence indicated that although Colonel Albert J. Fountain was killed during the ambush, his son was taken alive, and only killed the next day.

The public was left without answers to the questions:

- Who ambushed and killed Colonel Fountain?
- Who was willing to kill his young son in cold-blood after holding him captive for 24 hours?

The case was never solved. Two men were eventually tried for and acquitted of the crime.

The case file for the crime contains almost no information. There are no trial transcripts or witness testimonies. The only reports that exist today of the investigation of the case are these Pinkerton Reports, which were commissioned by the Territorial Governor, and then stolen from his office four months after the murders. These Reports, now recovered, are published here.

These Reports are important historical documents, not only for what they reveal about the Fountain murders, but also as a fascinating window into how the most famous professional detective agency in the United States in the 1890s - the Pinkerton Detective Agency - went about investigating a murder, at a time when scientific forensic evidence was virtually non-existent.

Printed in Great Britain
by Amazon